A LONG WAY FROM HOME

Evacuee Memories 80 Years On

Authors:

Sandra Delf & Clive Capps

Spring Daisy Press

British Library Cataloguing in Publication Data
A CIP catalogue record for this book is available from the British Library.

ISBN 978-1-9996030-1-4

Authors Disclaimer

These are true stories of the experiences and recollections of evacuees as told by them to the authors. The stories are entirely from the evacuee's subjective perspective and it is acknowledged that their interpretation of their story may not match exactly with the recollection of others.

It is the intention to tell how those children who were displaced by evacuation during WW2 were affected.

Designed and printed by
Century Printing, Stalham, Norfolk, NR12 9AZ
www.centuryprinting.co.uk

ACKNOWLEDGEMENTS

We would like to thank the following people for their help and support with creating this book.

All those WW2 evacuees who shared their memories with us.

Jo Wilde and the staff of Lowestoft Library for their considerable help and support.

Maurice Blick – Sculptor of Evacuees Memorial for the BEA.

The British Evacuee Association – James Roffey MBE and Karen Follows, manager and editor of 'Evacuee' magazine.

Chris Brooks – Secretary of the Lowestoft Evacuees Association.

Ivan Bunn – Local Lowestoft historian for his maps.

Century Printing, Stalham, Norfolk – Roger and Katie Newman.

Rose Chapman – Granddaughter of Lowestoft evacuee.

Bob Collis – Local Lowestoft historian.

Revd Philip Cudmore – Beccles Parish, son of evacuee.

Mark Gladding – Retired teacher and proof reader with an interest in the social impact of WW2.

Burt Collyer – All Our Yesterdays Picture Show.

Sarah Lovatt and the Lowestoft U3A Writers Group.

Pam Raven – Retired history teacher, daughter of Dagenham evacuee.

Megan Turner – Drawings of evacuee children.

Neil Williams – Friends of Glossop Station, instrumental in establishing a plaque on Glossop station to commemorate the arrival of Lowestoft evacuees.

GENERAL DEDICATION

This book is dedicated to all those WW2 evacuee children who because of the threat of bombing and invasion were sent away at short notice from their families and friends to safe places in the country.

In particular, the authors wish to acknowledge the determination and spirit shown by the 40 evacuees featured in the book, most in their late 80s and early 90s, who have looked back on their evacuation 80 years earlier and then gone on to briefly tell how their lives turned out after evacuation.

FOREWORD

I, James Roffey, founded the Evacuees Reunion Association (ERA) in 1996. As a former evacuee myself I was sent on 1st September, 1939 at the age of eight from Camberwell, South London to Pulborough, West Sussex. I enjoyed the countryside and became a 'country boy' who resented being back in London after the war.

I decided to take early retirement in 1991 at the age of 60 which gave me more time to think about my early childhood as an evacuee and the impact it had upon me. I managed to get a ticket for the Great Tribute and Promise Parade along the Mall in London, to celebrate the 50th Anniversary of the end of the Second World War. The response of the crowds to myself and my brother John, wearing our luggage labels prompted me to form the ERA. 'The Evacuee' today is a 16 page magazine which is sent to our 1300 members all over the world. We are the leading authority on the subject and frequently deal with requests for information from individuals, many themselves former evacuees, historical societies, programme makers and the media. The ERA, now renamed as The British Evacuees Association (BEA) continues to go from strength to strength.

I personally think it is a great idea to mark the 80th Anniversary of the Lowestoft evacuees leaving in June 1940 by collecting their experiences together to create this fascinating and informative book.

These former evacuees experienced the Second World War as children. The cruel nature of the War and all that it brought with it, meant that they were no longer safe in their own homes, confirmed later by severe damage from bombing of homes and schools in Lowestoft. They were taken to 'places of safety' and were not re-united with their families, in some cases, as in my own, until after the War had finished in 1945.

It is important that 80 years later this group of nearly 40 evacuees, have given these valuable and varying accounts of their wartime experiences which form a permanent record for future generations. This unique collection of stories echo what we already know to be, the good, the bad, the happy, and the sad memories of a long time ago.

James Roffey MBE

CONTENTS

THE DAGENHAM STORIES

THE LOWESTOFT STORIES

HOST VILLAGES & MORE STORIES

BRITISH EVACUEES ASSOCIATION (BEA)

The BEA, formerly The Evacuees Reunion Association, was formed in 1996 with the support of The Imperial War Museum in London and is a registered charity. It was founded by former evacuee James Roffey to provide an audible voice for WW2 children evacuees, previously known as the Silent Generation, because of their reluctance to reveal often painful wartime memories. Many evacuees have now disclosed their incredible wartime stories for posterity, so future generations can learn what it was like to be an evacuee separated from loved-ones, for sometimes months, years or, even forever. The evacuation process, often termed the greatest social upheaval in British history, involved the movement of 3.5 million people, the majority of which were children.

The BEA publishes a bi-monthly 16 page magazine 'The Evacuee' which is a 16 page publication full of stories, photographs, articles of interest, news of events and a 'Lost Touch' section. It is an invaluable source of information for educational establishments, various societies and those generations wanting to find out more about this important part of our British history. It aims to place on record the impact that evacuation had upon communities throughout the United Kingdom, not just those in the departure areas, but also those in the designated reception areas. It also records the stories of the evacuation of children from the UK to Canada, Australia, New Zealand and South Africa. Operated by the Children's Overseas Reception Board (CORB), it was a scheme that was brought to an abrupt and tragic end by the sinking of the carrier ship the SS City of Benares on the way to North America when it was torpedoed with significant loss of life, including the majority of the evacuees on board.

The BEA pays tribute, not just to the evacuees, but to everyone involved in the evacuation, such as the foster parents, teachers, nurses, train drivers and billeting officers. Membership is open to everyone and in 2020 there were around 1300 members worldwide, with an annual subscription cost of £28.

In July 2017 the BEA celebrated its 21st year by installing their National Memorial to the Evacuation which was dedicated by HRH The Duke of Gloucester, at The National Memorial Arboretum, New Litchfield in Staffordshire. This event was attended by over 220 members, family and friends and will be a permanent reminder to future generations as to the experiences of the evacuees. More details are given on page xiii – National Evacuees Memorial.

The BEA have also held events in Westminster Abbey (1999), St James' Park (2005), and St Pauls Cathedral (2009). The latter was the largest gathering to date when 1800 people comprising evacuees, family and friends, were present. The BEA are also represented in the annual Cenotaph Parade in London commemorating Remembrance Day.

BEA MANAGEMENT STRUCTURE

James Roffey MBE,
founder (retired)

Karen Follows,
Manager and Editor of
Evacuee Magazine

Patrons

Lord Carey of Clifton
Former Archbishop of Canterbury and evacuee

Mr Michael Aspel OBE
Television Presenter and former evacuee

Sir Robert Crawford CBE
Former Director General of the IWM

Mr Henry Sandon MBE
Television Presenter and former evacuee

Lady Emma Barnard
Parham Park, home for WW2 evacuees

The Late Sir Bruce Forsyth
Former patron and evacuee

The Late Sir Roger Moore
Former patron and evacuee

Karen Follows, the Manager of the BEA, joined the charity in January 2000. Now in her 21st year, she continues to be responsible for running the Association and became Editor of 'The Evacuee' magazine in 2013 after James retired. At the time of her appointment she herself had three children of school age, and was interested in the story of the evacuation. Over the years one of her duties has been the fundraising and planning for the installation of The National Memorial to the Evacuation at The National Memorial Arboretum in Staffordshire. She organised the dedication event on 25th July 2017 at which HRH The Duke of Gloucester and 220 former evacuees, family and friends were present. This significant event attracted worldwide attention and will ensure that the evacuation story will not be forgotten by future generations.

The BEA covers all aspects of the evacuation and the office receives numerous enquiries on a daily basis. Karen has successfully run the Association and maintained an active membership of over 1300 members worldwide. This is a commendable achievement considering the age of the membership (former evacuees) are now in their eighties and early nineties. The main focus of the Association remains to promote and raise awareness of the Evacuation story, which involved 3.5 million people in the UK, the majority of which were children.

NATIONAL EVACUEES MEMORIAL
'EVERY WHICH WAY'

Maurice Blik, sculptor PPRBS

Maurice Blik was born in Holland, and at the age of 5 was sent to Bergen Belsen Nazi camp where he became very aware of the feelings of being displaced. In 2005, the BEA had the idea to create a memorial to all WW2 evacuees and Maurice, a renowned sculptor was identified to produce this memorial in the form of a statue.

The statue depicted nine children of various ages, cast in bronze and standing alongside each other. At first glance they appear to be holding hands, closer inspection reveals that they are all separate, alone, as they often were, when they were sent away. Their faces and contorted limbs reflect the confusion and distress felt by many of them.

The opening ceremony organised by Karen Follows, manager of BEA, held in July 2017 was attended by over 200 people, mostly evacuees. The unveiling was carried out by the HRH Duke of Gloucester.

L to R, Prudence, Valour, Ernest, Hope, Faith, Defiance, Constance, Will, Resolute.

LOWESTOFT EVACUEES ASSOCIATION (LEA)

The LEA was founded in 1990 by Chris Brooks BSc, then a teacher at Roman Hill Middle School, Lowestoft and formerly a graduate of Kings College, London. He was inspired to establish the Association by Mrs Iris Smith, Head of Governors Roman Hill School who was herself an evacuee.

Lowestoft Evacuees Association (committee members), with chairman Chris Brooks, founder of LEA (circled)

Reunions took place every year in Lowestoft to mark the evacuation of the 3,000 Lowestoft school children in June 1940 to towns and villages in Derbyshire and Worksop in Nottinghamshire. This was part of a large-scale evacuation of close to 48,000 school children from East Coast towns because of the threat of invasion across the channel from the German occupied countries of Belgium and Holland.

These annual reunions in Lowestoft became very popular attracting each year up to the millennium well over 100 former evacuees from not just Lowestoft but also from other UK towns and even overseas.

In 2006, a committee was formed with Chris Brooks as Chairman and Clive Capps as secretary, assisted by a number of other dedicated former evacuees. Soon after, the committee organised annual visits by coach to the towns and villages where they had stayed and were met by local people, some of whom were children when the evacuees arrived in 1940.

Reunion at Stella Maris Hall 2017

Special events were planned for the 60th and 70th LEA anniversaries. Also a number of former evacuees from the LEA attended the national 70th evacuees anniversary at St. Pauls Cathedral, London in 2009 where over 1,500 former evacuees were present. By this time Brian Baxter had been appointed Chairman of the LEA.

In July 2017, Chris Brooks, as Secretary, represented LEA at the BEA event of the unveiling by HRH Duke of Gloucester, of the Evacuees Memorial 'Every Which Way' at the National Memorial Arboretum. He was presented to the Duke also meeting James Roffey, founder chairman of the BEA, Karen Follows, manager and a number of Patrons of the Association. The following year, Lowestoft members on the summer visit to Glossop by minibus, travelled via the Arboretum to view the memorial.

The 80th anniversary of the LEA will be marked by the production of a book of evacuee stories compiled by author Sandra Delf with co-author Clive Capps, former evacuee and Vice Chairman of the LEA. These stories were obtained by taped interviews of close to 40 evacuees and cover the range of experiences they went through some 80 years ago, both good and bad.

In order to ensure the reunions continue and evacuation story lives on, it is planned to establish a 'next generation' sub-committee which will consist of committee members of the LEA assisted by the grown up children and grandchildren of evacuees plus other interested parties.

IN MEMORIAM – A TRIBUTE

In the 80 years that have gone by since we were evacuated, regrettably a number of the evacuees have passed on. It is appropriate to remember those committee members that made that difference by the support they gave so willingly.

Joan Shrubsall (née Lawrence)
Evacuee 'Poet'

Joan was evacuated at the age of 7 from Roman Hill School, Lowestoft to Creswell, Derbyshire in June 1940. She joined the Lowestoft Evacuee Association in late 1990s and shortly after formed an evacuee sub group in Norwich jointly with Clive Capps. She was the life and soul of the party and was well known for the numerous poems she produced at the drop of a hat.

Derek Aldred   *DVD Wizard*

Derek was evacuated at the age of 11 from Gorleston Road School, Lowestoft to Barlborough, Derbyshire in June 1940. After the war he worked at Pye television factory for most of his life. On joining the Lowestoft Evacuee Association he spent much time, effort and expense to produce photo albums and video recordings covering the reunions and trips to host villages.

Owen Draper   *Bookkeeper*

Owen was evacuated at age 10 from Gorleston Road School, Lowestoft to Barlborough, Derbyshire in June 1940. He married Mary James, another evacuee and being older than Mary, looked after her and sister Violet on the 1940 train journey to Derbyshire. He joined the Lowestoft Evacuee Association in 2000 and right up until his passing acted as book-keeper for the Association.

INTRODUCTION

What was it like to be a child in the extraordinary times during WW2, spanning the years 1939 – 1945. This book gives an insight into the lives of some young evacuees (5 to 15 years old) in particular from Lowestoft but also including some from the Dagenham/Gravesend area through their own words. Their testimonies are a witness to how it felt and of the considerable upheaval they suffered. Eighty years have passed and it is important that their memories should be recorded before it is too late. The homes they went to are referred to as their billets and the people who looked after them as their foster parents. Also included are stories from the children of families who took in these evacuees.

Those who stayed at home, came face to face with the horrors of bombing raids and the consequent destruction from enemy aircraft. The children who were taken back home because they were placed in unsuitable billets or were homesick or unwell could have lost their lives because of it.

The Phoney War

The Phoney War was the period between the British declaration of war in September 1939 and the invasion of France and the Low Countries, by the Germans, in May 1940. In September 1939 evacuees from Dagenham and Gravesend arrived in Lowestoft and other East Coast ports. During the Phoney War things were quiet with no big bombing raids on Britain. This encouraged many evacuees to return home.

Once this period ended, Lowestoft being the most easterly point of the United Kingdom, thus out on a limb and with Holland occupied by the Germans, was only a thirty minute flight for the enemy. Lowestoft was therefore in the front line for hit and run attacks and even invasion.

Operation Pied Piper

Operation Pied Piper was the Government's code name for the evacuation scheme. It led to huge social upheaval tearing families apart.

The plan had mixed success with some evacuees having a very positive experience and others quite the opposite.

In May 1938, an Evacuation Committee was created. The Committee decided that if children where not evacuated, as part of their family they should be evacuated with their schools and be billeted in private houses in so-called safe reception areas. Children were seen as the future of the country and would be needed to re-build it after the war.

Operation Pied Piper - phase 1

At the time of the first wave of evacuation in September 1939, Lowestoft was considered to be a safe area.

> *"When plans were drawn up to take evacuees from the cities. Norfolk, Suffolk and Essex were to receive 50,000 London evacuees each. These plans changed . . ."* [1]

The Women's Voluntary Service *(WVS)* were charged with conducting a survey to determine how many places were available for evacuees in each area. They were not always welcome on the doorstep. Hosts were required to accept a child, or children, depending on the number of available rooms in their homes. Host families were compensated with a payment and sometimes this was the motive for taking in children. This was *'10s 6d a week for a single child taken in or 8s 6d for each of two or more children...'* [2]

The government gave local authorities the power to make householders take in evacuees. Some householders refused and were taken to court and fined. Evacuee children were sometimes used as cheap farm labour. However, many were treated well.

The parents did have a choice, unlike the accompanying teachers, for whom evacuation was compulsory, unless they were eligible to be called up for active service. The teachers, too, were experiencing upheaval. Those teachers who accompanied the children, took on a huge responsibility.

---

[1] East Coast Evacuees page 3 Chris Brooks
[2] East Coast Evacuees page 24 Chris Brooks

On the 13th October 1940 on BBC Children's Hour, Princess Elizabeth (now the Queen), at the age of 14 with her sister Princess Margaret, aged 10, sitting beside her, made her first public speech with a radio address for children in the United Kingdom and overseas who had been separated from their families.

Operation Pied Piper phase 2

"In 1940 the coastal strip of East Anglia was declared to be a possible invasion zone." On Sunday 2nd June 1940 five trains left Lowestoft Central Railway Station taking around 3,000 children plus teachers to their evacuation destinations in Derbyshire and Nottinghamshire. Some had been told that they were going on a great adventure.

The children who had been evacuated to Lowestoft in 1939 from the London area had already been moved to billets elsewhere.

The Derbyshire towns and villages received little notice that they would receive an influx of evacuees from the Lowestoft area. The families of the children were putting their trust in the authorities and the receiving families. The children were forced to adjust to separation from family and friends and sometimes there was a large cultural difference between the evacuees and their host families. On arrival, many children found being 'chosen' (or otherwise) by a host family a traumatic event. Often foster parents chose the children they liked the look of. It is said that in some cases people haggled over the most presentable children.

Most of the evacuee stories in this book have been, unless otherwise stated, given directly by the evacuee. These contributing evacuees were interviewed by myself and Clive Capps using a voice recorder and their stories were produced from there. These were then carefully checked for accuracy and then read back to the evacuee to check that it was a true record of their story. One or two evacuees have written their own account and these have been acknowledged, where applicable.

I have already published 'Keep Smiling Through' – letters written by my father from prisoner of war camps during WW2. This book is an acknowledgement of another group, this time as children, whose stories may be seen as secondary to those who were away fighting and lost in battle. However, the evacuation story is also one of considerable suffering and upheaval

We will now leave it to the evacuees to tell their own stories.

Sandra Delf

EVACUATION TIMELINE FOR WORLD WAR 2

Events connected to evacuation in particular with regard to evacuees from Lowestoft and Dagenham .

May 1938

An evacuation committee was established to consider the evacuation of school children from unsafe areas in the event of war breaking out. The Women's Voluntary Service (WVS) carried out house-to-house surveys in reception areas to find out how many places were available for evacuees.

15th April 1939

The first test of the 'black-out' in Lowestoft took place.

May 1939

Parents who wished their children to be evacuated were told to register at their school.

Summer 1939

Schools held rehearsals for evacuee departure day.

August 1939

A Ministry of Health broadcast notified teachers in evacuation areas that they should return to their districts and report to their schools.

31st August 1939

At 11.07am the order was given to evacuate forthwith.

THE FIRST WAVE OF EVACUATION – Threat of bombing

1st September 1939

The evacuation of 16,000 Dagenham and Gravesend school children to Lowestoft and other East Coast ports by sea over a three day period.

2nd September 1939

A request appeared in the Lowestoft Journal for volunteers to assist with the schoolchildren evacuated to Lowestoft.

11.15am Sunday 3rd September 1939.

The Prime Minister announced that Britain was at war with Germany.

26th May 1940

'The Minister of Health, Malcolm MacDonald, announced that as Holland and parts of Belgium and Northern France were in enemy occupation, the government had decided that a large number of towns on the East and South-East coast be declared evacuation areas.' [1]

June 1st 1940

An announcement was made in the press of the decision to remove evacuated children from rural or urban areas within approximately ten miles of the coast of Suffolk, Essex, Kent, and parts of Norfolk. No more children to be evacuated to these areas.

SECOND WAVE – Threat of Invasion

June 2nd 1940
Over 3,000 children were evacuated from Lowestoft to Derbyshire and Nottinghamshire.

September 1940
The so-called Blitz of London began.

June 13th 1941
The Lowestoft Central School was bombed.

13th January 1942
Lowestoft's worst air-raid of World War 2 took place. This became known as 'The Waller's Raid.'

12th May 1943
The Lowestoft Wilde's School was bombed.

8th May 1945
V-E Day (Victory in Europe) the end of World War Two.

---

[1] Page 24 East Coast Evacuees by Chris Brooks

April 1945

The Government began to make travel arrangements to return the evacuees to their homes.

15th August 1945

Victory over Japan. Victory in the Pacific.

WW2 BOMBARDMENT OF LOWESTOFT

A Contribution from local historian Bob Collis

Traumatised by the reports of wholesale destruction and mass casualties in the Spanish civil War in 1937, the British government were under no delusions as to what the full force of the rapidly growing Luftwaffe would achieve if unleashed against Britain.

Some evacuees were actually aboard steamers en route to Lowestoft and other east coast locations when Prime Minister Neville Chamberlain's famous 'War with Germany' speech was broadcast. In fact it was not until after the fall of France in June 1940, that the Luftwaffe began widespread bombing in Great Britain. Huge stockpiles of cardboard coffins for the victims of the anticipated onslaught went unused.

Lowestoft was attacked for a variety of reasons. Firstly its geographical location, being 100 miles or 20 minutes flying time from occupied Holland and the Luftwaffe bases there. It was a well-known location with several easily distinguishable landmarks for navigation. Any location with a military presence was a potential target and Lowestoft had the RNPS Central Depot HMS 'Europa.' There was also a considerable force of minelayer/minesweeper/Coastal Forces MTB/MGBs in port here.

It took a long time before any heavy AA guns were sited in Lowestoft. Up until January 1941 when the first dedicated AA unit arrived, Lowestoft had been defended by four LMGs[1]. Heavy guns were not sited in the town until October 1941 by which time the 'hit and run' attacks had passed their peak.

Lowestoft's first air raid 'alert' sounded at 11.45 am on Sunday 3 Sept 1939, a mere 30 minutes after Prime Minister Neville Chamberlain made his famous speech declaring war with Nazi Germany and just 59 days after the Lowestoft evacuees left. It was variously stated to have been a test or a misidentified civilian aircraft approaching Croydon Airport.

---

[1] Light Machine guns

The first bombs dropped in Lowestoft in the early hours of 21 June 1940. It was to be the first of 105 air raids which were to cause immense damage and casualties.

There were periods during the winter and spring of 1940-41 when continuous intermittent raid warnings made normal life impossible. Some people simply refused to take shelter, a stoic British attitude which sometimes cost lives.

The cumulative damage inflicted by 'hit-and-run' attacks in the early part of 1941 was considerable. Some buildings were damaged by bombs on four or five occasions and a number of well-known Lowestoft landmarks disappeared from the skyline.

D-Day came and went and people were beginning to think the end was in sight. It proved a false dawn because then came the V-1 Flying Bomb or 'Doodlebug.' Thousands of these pilot-less, jet-propelled missiles were sent across the Channel and North Sea during the summer of 1944.

The final statistics make grim reading. Out of 11,830 houses in the borough in 1939, no fewer than 9,433 in number had been damaged to some extent. By October 1944 by which time the only enemy action was V-1 Flying Bombs, it was reported that 50 acres of bomb damaged buildings had been cleared by demolition and that repairs to 13,379 houses had been carried out. The same report stated 494 houses had been completely destroyed along with 76 shops and business premises and seven large public buildings which included Central School, Wilde's School, the Carnegie Free Library and two churches.

The missiles dropped by the Luftwaffe on the town and surrounding district comprised a staggering 992 HE bombs[2] and more than 18,000 incendiary bombs. Property could be replaced; people could not. The bombing claimed the lives of 192 civilians and 83 service personnel. 731 people were injured.

During the 2,075 days of war the Lowestoft air-raid warning system operated 2,064 times – a total unsurpassed by any other location in Britain.

---

[2] High Explosive bombs

Central School after bombing 13 June 1941

Wilde's School after bombing 12 May 1943

Photos from the Burt Collyer Collection

EVACUATION OF DAGENHAM SCHOOL CHILDREN

(Written by Pam Raven, daughter of evacuee Evelyn Rowe)

INTRODUCTION

Why a target for the Germans?

Situated on the Thames, Dagenham had been home to small industries as early as the 1800s and in 1887 Samuel Williams bought the site of the Dagenham (Thames) Dock Company and began development of the Dagenham Thames Bank. 1908 saw the building of the Dagenham Dock Railway Station, with direct links to East London, and the establishment of cable-making, commercial spirit, rope-making and batteries industries.

Ford Motor Company, Dagenham was formed on 7 December 1928 with the purchase of 244 acres from Samuel Williams and work on factory started in 1929. May and Baker, a chemicals industry, was established in Dagenham in 1934 and associated industries grew in the area.

By 1939, the extent of industry, increased size of the population to approximately 93,000 and its close proximity to London made Dagenham a likely target in the event of enemy action.

The approach to government

The Civil Defence Act of 1939 led to the country being divided into evacuation, reception and neutral areas and when the general evacuation scheme was announced by the Minister of Health, Dagenham was listed as a neutral area.

John Gerard O'Leary, Dagenham's Chief Librarian and local historian, records[1] that, 'a protest was addressed to the Ministry on 11 January 1939, and a deputation consisting of the Mayor, Alderman, and Officers, was received at the Ministry on 31 January. On 13 June 1939, the Ministry of Health informed the Borough Council that Dagenham was now an evacuable area'.

---

[1] Danger Over Dagenham by John G O'Leary 1947. Re-printed 2018

Involvement of shipping company that provided the paddle steamers

By mid- August 1939, plans and arrangements for London were practically completed but the local situation for Dagenham was very uncertain and it was clear that the Ministry was concerned regarding travel and billeting arrangements. O'Leary notes that uncertainty was 'cleared by a suggestion from the Directors of the General Steam Navigation Company who suggested the transport of evacuees from the Riverside boroughs to coastal resort in their boats'. The suggestion was adopted and on the Monday before evacuation began, the scheme was announced and registration began with the plan being that on the day of evacuation, parties of schoolchildren with teachers and helpers would assemble at an assigned school. Ford Motor Company offered their jetties to berth the steamers: Royal Eagle, Crested Eagle, Golden Eagle, Royal Sovereign, Queen of the Channel, Medway Queen, City of Rochester, and Laguna Belle. The total loading capacity for each sailing of all the boats was 11,902.

On Thursday 27 August instructions were received to proceed with the evacuation. Records show that a total of nearly 17,000 registrations were made for evacuation from Dagenham.

Make up of passengers in paddle steamers provided by Central Steam Navigation Co

School Children	7,248
Non-School Parties, Adults	2,294
Non-School Parties, Children	4,633
Expectant Mothers	290
Teachers	666
Helpers	266
Late Registrations	1,587
TOTAL	**16,984**

The first sailing left Dagenham on 1 September with Ministry of Health instructions being received the following day that total numbers should not exceed 20,292 otherwise there would not be enough billets in Norfolk and Suffolk. O'Leary notes that arrangements for reception at Great Yarmouth and Felixstowe were 'in the hands of the Ministry and local reception officials – plans were not made known to us'. The suddenness of the exodus from Dagenham meant reception authorities had little time to prepare and, in addition, Great Yarmouth was in a neutral position until quite late when it was declared as a reception area.

The following accounts are from evacuees who actually sailed from Dagenham to Suffolk and Norfolk coastal towns in early September 1939.

Dennis Gammon was six years old in 1939 when he arrived in Lowestoft from Dagenham on board the evacuee ship the Royal Eagle.

THEY WERE AFRAID OF US MESSING UP THE HOUSE

Dennis on the left

At the outbreak of war in September 1939, on evacuation day, I was sent off with my eleven year old sister, Elsie, with my gas mask, a bag containing an apple, orange and a piece of cake. I was 6 years old, the youngest of three children, and attending Finimore School, Dagenham.

We went by coach to Dagenham dock where there were lots of children lined up. We boarded the Royal Eagle ship to Lowestoft. On the journey, not many children cried as they were all too interested in the ship. Unbeknown to me, my future wife Pamela was also aboard that same ship.

I found out, later, that this trip by sea was just one part of a major operation organised by the government to evacuate over 19,000 children from the London area to the coastal towns of Felixstowe, Lowestoft and Great Yarmouth.

The Royal Eagle was a paddle steamer, originally intended to provide excursion holidays from London to Ramsgate, Southend, and Margate.

It was built in 1930 by Cammell Laird at Birkenhead and was capable of carrying 2,000 passengers and crew. After this evacuation operation, it was used in the war effort for the Dunkirk evacuation and eventually was scrapped in 1954. It was built as part of the Eagle series named Golden Eagle, Crested Eagle, and finally Royal Eagle.

Altogether I had three billets and in each case, when a change was made, I went back home for a short while to Dagenham.

Lowestoft
When the ship docked at Lowestoft we went to a big hall in Corton, just north of Lowestoft. One of the boys, Eddie Kirkham, whose house had been bombed, was tough and the only one not crying. We slept there for two nights on straw beds. After being 'selected', I stayed for a few months in Lowestoft with someone called Elsie. When it became evident that she was pregnant, we were sent home.

Letcombe Bassett, Berks
I then was sent to Berkshire, to Letcombe Bassett, where we were with Mrs Garland for one year. Mr Garland worked on a farm. We were away from the war, that was the main thing. You didn't think of the danger as children. When we went back home the doodle bugs were starting.

Peasmore, Berks
Next, I was sent to Peasmore in Berkshire with two other boys about the same age, Eddie Kirkham and a boy called Len. When we were 'chosen', we were in a hall.

In Peasmore we were billeted in a large house with two spinsters, Miss Millie and Miss Sophie. We were there for two years. My sister lived at the Post Office at the other end of the village with Mrs Print and her husband. He was a farrier and she looked after the shop.

In the back garden there was a mound of earth. Myself and another boy dug it up thinking we had done a marvellous job. We thought we had found treasure. But we had dug up 10 gallons of petrol Miss Millie and Miss Sophie had buried just in case the Germans came. We got into trouble for that.

We used to have breakfast in the kitchen but, for main meals we ate outside because they were afraid of us messing up the house. Bearing in mind they were two elderly spinsters and we were three boys from London, we must have driven them potty. I remember in the bedroom in the roof there was a house martin's nest and we didn't know what it was and she said, 'You silly boys, it's a bird's nest.'

We had a pleasant time there. The two old ladies had a car and we used to go to Wantage. That was the biggest nearby town. I can remember going to the cinema once. That was our treat. There were no bombs or anything there because it was such a small place.

They had a maid called Gwen, who was in her teens. I fell in love with her. I thought she was the most marvellous thing I had ever seen. But it all stopped when I heard her swear. I wasn't used to that. I went back to visit after the war, with Pam, my wife. Gwen was still going strong and she still had all her fingernails and toenails painted and had just renewed her driving licence. She recognised me.

Miss Millie was also still alive but quite old by the time we went back. She had moved out of the big house into a bungalow. I think she had some idea of who I was.

I have a photo taken after coming home when I was about twelve on a school outing. We were driving an American mad, following him around in Kew Gardens, saying to him, 'Have you got any gum chum?' He took a photo of us which he sent to us later. Because of our young years we didn't reciprocate. On the back he had put his rank. I have often thought I could send it to the American Airforce base to find out who he was.

When I was about twelve, towards the end of the war, and back home, my mother would often take me to my aunt's where we stayed overnight. My sister used to sleep in the back room of the house. A rocket came down 300 yards away. My mother couldn't get home quick enough. She took my hand and we ran down Gale Street. My sister was there and she was OK. My mother's bed head, which was wooden, had a million splinters of glass in it. If my sister had been in it she would have been killed. My father was on night work at the time. He was in

WW1 and too old for WW2. He worked at the Ford Motor Company, and he was a good old dad.

After the war I bought a scooter, a Vespa. At one of the scooter club meetings at the Royal Oak in Romford, my future wife, Pam, turned up on the back of her friend's scooter. We got married four years later and my brother was best man.

Pam and I didn't realise till later that we had both been on that same evacuee ship, the Royal Eagle, from Dagenham to Lowestoft. Also, our homes were originally just 3 miles apart in Dagenham – all quite incredible but a very happy ending.

Pam Gammon, (née Gregory), was eight years old when she was evacuated from Dagenham to Lowestoft in 1939, then re-evacuated to West Beckham, near Holt in Norfolk.

THE GOOD LORD ALREADY AT WORK

Pam sitting on the bike

I was the youngest of five children. I went to Alibon Junior School, Dagenham and was eight years old when we were evacuated. My brother, Len, was eleven. We were taken to the docks and boarded the Royal Eagle, which took us to Lowestoft. I overheard my father saying at the quayside to Len, 'Now look after that girl as she is much younger than you,' and he certainly did! I remember we were each given a paper bag with basic provisions such as apple, biscuits and cake.

I think I stayed a while in Lowestoft. After a short time, it was decided, by the government, that Lowestoft was no longer a safe haven, so we were re-evacuated.

So my brother, Len, and I, were evacuated to a tiny village called West Beckham, near Holt, Norfolk. Our foster mother, Mrs Ford, had two adopted daughters, Doris and Margaret. Doris was really her 'help'. She was about twenty-three at the time. Mrs Ford was about fifty and always wore a long black dress and had her grey hair back in a bun.

I can remember coming home from school with my brother once and he had just learnt where babies came from and on the way home he told me. At the meal table he asked me that same question and I said, Out of mummy's tummy. Poor Mrs Ford, she was just coming in with a plate of dumplings - we lived on dumplings, which were delicious - and she dropped the dumplings on her lap, saying, 'What would your mother say?'

Doris got on very well with my brother and overall we had a happy time there. We kept in touch with them after the war and visited and Len would take them out. Sometimes we used to take a barrow and walk to Sheringham and pick up bits of wood for the fire. We walked miles. There was a pump outside the cottage for water and the toilet was down the garden. I am not sure why, but for a short time we were sent to Cheadle near Manchester

Mum and Dad came to visit us as often as they could. I have a photograph of one of these times. Father fought in the First World War and after that worked at Shell. He was a professional chemist and spent some time with the army in Egypt (before I was born). One of my other brothers, Ron, was called up into the Forces and unfortunately ended up in a Stalag as a prisoner of war.

When I came home, before the war had finally ended, I was upstairs when the first doodle bug came over. You heard it, the sound would stop and you would know they are falling.

I met my husband, Dennis, at the Vespa Club in Romford. However, it was some while after we met that I realised I was on the Royal Eagle, aged eight, as an evacuee travelling to Lowestoft, at the same time as my future husband, then aged six. I now know that the good Lord was already at work. We were married in 1960.

Dennis and I went back to see Mrs Ford again after we were married but unfortunately she had died. However, we still kept in touch with Doris.

Doris and her husband Bob

Evelyn Rowe (1926-2008) was evacuated twice during WW2 with her younger sister Iris. In the 1970s she wrote a comprehensive account of her experiences and what follows is an extract describing the evacuation from Dagenham to Lowestoft at the outbreak of war which her daughter, Pam Raven, has kindly shared with us.

WE SLEPT ON STRAW

Evelyn with sister Iris (left), at Dagenham in July 1939

'It was Friday, September 1st: my sister Iris and I were woken by Mother at 4 a.m. The year was 1939 and war was imminent. We were to be evacuated that day to a safe area. Until quite recently, Dagenham hadn't been considered to be in the danger-zone, so the preparations appeared to be somewhat hasty (at least that's what we thought at the time).

We'd been issued with gas masks some time before the war broke out. The air-raid wardens called at each house to measure everyone for size. We had fun trying on the gas masks! They were not very comfortable and soon became hot and sticky as the eye-screen misted over. It amused us that if we laughed or even breathed a bit heavy, they made rather rude noises!

To prepare for evacuation, we'd been instructed to limit our luggage to one small bag each, containing one change of clothes, nightwear and food for the journey. Our haversacks were gas mask cases from the

First World War with the centre sections removed. They were army issue, made of strong canvas and just about big enough to hold what we needed with straps attached so that we could carry them on our backs leaving our hands free.

We had to be at school by five a.m. After breakfast we kissed Dad goodbye and Mum accompanied us to school. It was my school (Marley) as Iris was still in Junior school (Marsh Green). Any junior pupil with older siblings in senior school, went with them to keep families together.

At school, we were assembled into groups and each teacher, who was to go with us, was allocated a group to take care of throughout the journey. I remember our teacher very well, although I'm not now too sure of her name. She was a Scottish lady who was accompanied by her own four-year-old son, Malcolm, who was wearing a kilt. She was very kind and took great care of us all.

When everyone was present, we marched down Ballards Road towards Kent Avenue where we met up with all the children and teachers from the junior school near the gates of Briggs Motor Bodies. We stood there for a while and then it was time to say goodbye to parents. It must have been harder for the parents than for us, no-one seemed to know where we were going.

The time must have been around 7 a.m. We moved off again and eventually came to Ford's jetty, where two paddle steamers were waiting. These had been used as pleasure boats on the Thames. The younger children boarded the 'Royal Daffodil' and the rest of us went on the older and smaller 'Royal Eagle'.

It was to be a long journey - about eight hours. We sailed down the Thames to the estuary and then into the North Sea. I don't remember what the weather was like except that it must have been dry as we were able to sit on the deck.

Most of the children seemed to enjoy the trip, exploring the boat, running around the decks and generally having fun – occasionally making nuisances of themselves with the crew! I didn't enjoy the journey at all as I was sea-sick and feeling quite miserable most of the way. I wasn't the only one, judging by the state of the toilet floors! I spent a lot of time sitting in a deckchair until finally the sickness wore off and I even managed to eat the ham sandwiches my Mother had packed for me. Iris had enjoyed the whole trip; I didn't see much of her and, when I did, she appeared to be having a great time with her friends.

It was a great relief to me when the boat finally docked at Lowestoft at about 4.30 p.m. Each teacher gathered their charges and we disembarked. We boarded waiting coaches and were driven to a local school. We were taken into classrooms which had been emptied of desks and the school's headmaster explained to us that this was where we'd be spending the night. He indicated some piles of straw in the corner and told us how, when he was a boy, he'd found it 'great fun' to sleep on straw. I'm not sure who he was trying to convince but we all dutifully gathered our own little heaps and made our beds. Iris and I put ours side by side, we used our coats as covers. It had been a very long day and we must all have been pretty tired, so were ready for sleep, even in our make-shift beds. We slept on straw but I don't remember being too uncomfortable!

We didn't realise it then, but we were to spend four nights at the school sleeping on our straw beds. I don't think anyone had expected that we would be staying that long, as little provision had been made for feeding us. We were each given one slice of bread, a small piece of cheese and half an apple - three times a day. On Sunday we all received a cup of soup, which hardly any of us drank. I remember how we queued to throw it down the lavatory. We were an ungrateful lot as someone must have taken the trouble to make it for us!

During the days that followed, we were able to go out, the first thing we had to do was send post-cards home to let our parents know where we were, although we still didn't know our final destination.

We were allowed to go out unaccompanied most of the time and we used to go out with Edna and Maisie, sisters who lived in our street at home. We made friends with a lady who lived in a house opposite the school. Her name was Mrs. Hughes and she had a daughter, Joy, who was about my age. Joy gave me a book 'Babes of the Wild' which I still have. The friendship she gave us was just what we needed in those early days away from our homes and parents.

On Sunday the third of September, whilst we were playing in the playground, someone came to tell us that war had been declared. The teachers had heard it on Chamberlain's radio broadcast to the nation. On hearing the news, a lot of the children were frightened and some began to cry. Quite soon after the declaration, the air raid sirens were sounded which only added to the panic.

All the teachers were wonderful during our time in Lowestoft. Some months later I heard one of them telling my Mother that the children had been very good so perhaps we helped each other. I know our parents must have worried, not knowing where we were. It would have been Monday before they received our postcards and even then, they didn't know where we were going from Lowestoft. Our teacher's sleeping arrangements weren't any better than ours, I went to the staff room one evening and found them settled into wooden armchairs. They didn't even have straw!

One day, one of the boys fell from the top of a cliff to the beach below and was badly injured. We were all very upset, the teachers tried to keep it from us, but it was rumoured that he later died.

We were told that we'd be leaving on Monday, so I sent another postcard home to let Mum and Dad know. In fact, this didn't happen and that evening, we heard that we would definitely be going Tuesday morning. On 5th September after breakfast, we were each given a paper carrier bag containing biscuits, a tin of corned beef, a tin of condensed milk and a big bar of chocolate. There may have been other items, but I've since forgotten. This food was meant to be given to the people with whom we were to be billeted – just in case they weren't prepared for our arrival!'

From top to bottom, sister Iris, Edna and Maisie
in Suffolk, 1939 - taken by Evelyn

POSTSCRIPT

Evelyn and Iris were billeted in Leiston, Suffolk until late December 1939 when they returned home to Dagenham. In 1940 when the Blitz began, they were evacuated to Shepton Mallet in Somerset.

Evelyn lived in Dagenham for the rest of her life. She met her husband William Milne in 1946 at the Briggs Motor Body plant where they worked after the war. They married on Saturday 13th September 1947, exactly a year after their first date, in the parish church of St Peter & St Paul in Dagenham. Mum always challenged the idea that Friday the 13th was an unlucky day!

Evelyn had three children (Robert, Pam and Colin), eight grandchildren and ten great-grandchildren. She travelled widely, much of it accompanying William who worked as a Trades Union Leader. She had a strong interest in family history, spending many hours searching the archives at Somerset House. She also retained an interest in the evacuation process by being a member of the British Evacuation Association until her death in 2008. Iris died in Cornwall on 1st January 2020 aged 90.

Pam Raven

Vera Grigg (née Legon) was just eight years old when she was evacuated from Fanshawe School in Dagenham on 2nd September 1939, the day before War was declared on Germany. The first stage of her journey was by sea in a paddle steamer to Great Yarmouth and then within a few days she was transferred to East Dereham in Norfolk.

DAGENHAM EVACUATION

The story has been well told of 'Pied Piper', the evacuation of London children before World War II started on 3rd September 1939. What is not so well known is how Dagenham children were evacuated.

When the details of the 'Pied Piper' organisation was announced, it was greeted with disbelief by my parents and many others in Dagenham, as their children were not included. Immediately, my father, William Frederick Legon, who was at that time an Alderman on the Council, together with other Council members, asked to see their MP, John Parker, at the House of Commons. They saw him and pointed out that Dagenham had Ford Works, Sterling Works, May and Baker, plus other engineering works, which were inevitably going to be the focus of German bombers. Therefore it was imperative that Dagenham children should be evacuated. John Parker followed up this request but his reply was that all trains were detailed to take London children, so therefore, Dagenham children could not be moved.

Soon after this was made public, the owner of the Pleasure Steamers that plied between the East Coast and Kent, offered all his steamers for the evacuation of Dagenham children.

That was how it was that on 31st August, the day before War was declared, I met up with my class at Fanshawe School in Parsloes Avenue very early in the morning. It was very exciting though I was aggrieved that only the Infants had transport to Dagenham Dock, we had to walk. I was then just eight years old and about to join the Juniors. We walked as a Class with our teacher, and boarded the 'Queen of the Channel' paddle steamer. It was a beautiful day, clear blue sky and the sea was flat. We, like all children, had a wonderful time, racing round the decks and exploring. I knew that we were being evacuated for the war effort, and my mother was helping on another boat. She landed at Lowestoft, together with the children she was looking after, while we landed at Great Yarmouth. We stayed overnight in the hall of a school that looked straight out onto the beach, but it was late, so we slept on straw palliases. Next morning we were taken by coach to East Dereham where I and a friend were billeted with a butcher and his wife right in the market square. We were wonderfully well looked after.

We had school for half a day, and our teacher took us on walks in the country for the other half.

Unfortunately, the butcher and his wife were Italians, and were subsequently interned and we were moved to a chicken farm. I was there for that very hard winter. I had never seen people skating on lakes before, and I remember the snow piled up so high as we walked to school that we could not see the fields.

My parents brought me home after the 'Phoney War' and I stayed in Dagenham for the remainder of the War. We were bombed twice, the first was a High Explosive in which my father was killed, and the second was a Doodlebug which destroyed the house. There was no school of course until near the end of the War, and I followed my mother around as she was in charge of all the Rest Centres in Dagenham. In particular, she was in charge of the one at Halbutt Street. Rest Centres were the place that those who were bombed out went to where they were provided a place of shelter, meals, clothing and a place to sleep until they were rehoused. My brother and sister, much older than I, were in the forces; my brother in the Fleet Air Arm and my sister in the Wrens.

So VE day has meant a very great deal to me, I remember the relief when we knew that the War was over, no more bombing and the family being able to be together again.

BEYOND EVACUATION

School restarted for my last year in the Juniors, and I passed the 'Scholarship' and then went to Dagenham County High, where I stayed for six years. I trained as a teacher at Leicester College of Domestic Subjects and subsequently gained a degree, studying evenings at Birkbeck College, then with the Open University. I gained a Master's Degree in London. My teaching experience was in Hornchurch, Walthamstow and Tower Hamlets, finally as a Head Teacher. I then moved into the Inspectorate and was an Ofsted Inspector for twelve years, finishing when I was 76.

In the following years of retirement I have kept my interest in education by being a School Governor. Until the 'Lockdown' I was a 'Patient Representative' for NELFT on interviewing teams.

On the 'Home Front', I married and had three children. My husband was a New Zealander teacher and we spent three years there, otherwise we have always lived in Essex. We enjoyed holidays around the World, mostly walking holidays. My last was early this year when I joined a son in New Zealand.

I always join the Evacuees group who march in Whitehall on Remembrance Sunday. The most amazing and wonderful experience was last year when I represented the Evacuees at the Royal British

Legion at the Festival of Remembrance at the Albert Hall. This was the first time that the Evacuees Association had been asked to send a representative – a very great honour.

Vera M Grigg (née Legon)

Marjorie Chilvers, (née Parker), was ten years old, and attending Lovewell Road School, when she and her younger sister, Myrtle, were evacuated to Glossop in Derbyshire. Her brother, Alan, was five years younger than her and stayed at home.

MOVED UP IN THE WORLD!

Marjorie

My sister, Myrtle, and I kept crazing our mum to allow us be evacuated. We said everyone else was going and we wanted to go. I don't know what we thought we were going to.

I can remember that day as clear as if it was yesterday. We got ready to be evacuated. We had our little attaché case and gas mask. We went out of the door and said cheerio to our mum and little brother, Alan. We walked down the road with Dad. I remember there was a post box a fair way down the road. At the post box, we turned round and waved. They waved back and off we went.

When we got to the school, because we were in different classes, I went one way and Myrtle went in another. When I got on the train, I didn't know where Myrtle was.

We had our cases and I remember one poor little girl, named Monica, didn't have a case. She only had a brown paper bag with a string handle.

She couldn't have had any clothes with her. Poor Monica didn't have anything for lunch so we all gave her one of our sandwiches

Every time the train came to a station, when it stopped we put the window of the door down and shouted, 'Are we there Mister?' Someone would say, 'No you're not there yet.' I don't know how many times we did that.

When we got to Glossop, we lined up, walked out of the station, and went to the market place, where we were given a bun and a drink. We were then taken to a hall, where people came in, picked children out, and took them away. I didn't see my sister. In the end, I was the only one sitting there. I was a 'little old' ginger girl, with straight hair. I suppose I wasn't very attractive. I can remember a lady saying, 'I'll take her', in a Derbyshire accent. So, off I went with her. We got to her house and she said to me that I should write a little note to my mum and dad to say I was there. She gave me her address. I didn't understand a lot of what she was saying. I kept saying, 'pardon'. It was like being in a foreign land to me. Anyway, I said that I had got a sister and didn't know where she was. She said, 'Never mind we'll go and see if we can find her tomorrow.'

The next day, we went out, I don't know how she found her, but we ended up where my sister was, at the other end of the village. The lady there, Mrs Pope, said she would take me as well. After a few weeks, we were told that we were moving somewhere else but would stay together. We went to Talbot House. It was only next door, but round the corner. Mrs Pope's garden and Talbot House garden met at the back.[1]

Talbot House was huge. It was where Lady Partington lived. We were the only evacuees there and the house was a bit bewildering. Lady Partington, we gathered, owned some of the local mills. She had servants: Bertha the cook, Nelly the laundry maid, Ethel the Lady's

---

[1] Talbot House, Talbot Road, Glossop. A grand Victorian property with substantial grounds built in 1855. Google 27.9.19

maid, Ellen the housemaid, Muriel the pantry maid, two gardeners, and a chauffeur. We had moved up in the world!

The house was divided into two. One half was where the maids lived and we lived there. In that half, we would go up a little staircase to a bedroom that Myrtle and I shared. The maids all had a bedroom. Through a door was the other half of the house, with a great, big, wide staircase. That other half was where 'M'lady' lived.

The house had six bathrooms, a huge drawing room, a huge dining room, and a billiard room with a full billiard table. There were gardens on three levels and trees on one side.

We had everything we could possibly need. There was nothing that we went without. At Christmas, we had parties. Mum and Dad came up every year at Christmas, for a fortnight.

We didn't have to do any work but sometimes I would take 'M'lady' her breakfast in bed. We also waited on guests at dinner parties. Nelly, the laundry maid, made us a little uniform, with a hat for when we did this. We liked it because some people were generous and gave us pocket money. The singers Pearl Carr and Teddy Johnson stayed there once.

We got lots of snow and there was a field next to the house. Bertha, the cook, used to let us have tin trays and we would sit on them and ride down the hill.

Alfie, the chauffeur, took us to where a bomb had dropped up in the hills and made a crater. Lots of people went to see that crater. Another weekend, we went to where they flooded a village, to make Derwent Water. They said it would be the last weekend that you would be able to see the village.

We went to West End School in Glossop. To start with, we either went in the morning or the afternoon, because they couldn't cope with all the children at once. I got on well with the local children. We had plenty of friends because they all wanted to come to the big house. As we were living there, we just took it for granted. We were lucky.

Many children had a very difficult time. Some were forced to do a lot of scrubbing of flagstone floors.

On the way to school we used to call for a girl called Molly. The Headmaster lived opposite her. If it was wet, we used to wait till we saw him get his car out, then we would start walking down the road. Of course, when he saw us he would give us a lift. We would time it just right!

The classroom doors had a glass panel at the top half. If I had been sent out of the classroom, for misbehaving, I used to stand outside the door and make faces through the glass. That meant I would have to go and stand outside the Headmaster's door. He would say, 'Marjorie! Not again'. I got to know him quite well! One of the teachers wacked my hand with the ruler once. I said, 'I've got handles to my cups, and saucers to match'. Out I had to go for being cheeky.

I stayed at Talbot House for the whole time I was away but my sister was clever and went to the Grammar school at Worksop, for the last year. This meant she moved to Worksop. I took the first part of the scholarship exam but was the wrong age to take the second part. Therefore, I didn't get a chance to finish it and went to the Central School in Hadfield.

I was fifteen when I came back. After all that luxury, when I came back home, our house, in Blackheath Road, felt like a shed with an outside toilet! We had also been used to a garden the size of Kensington Gardens, a park in Lowestoft. I can remember more about going away, than coming back. Lady Partington was an elderly lady and she died just after we came back home. Being evacuated was a good experience.

I got a job in the office of Morton's factory and married Ronald. Ronald worked on the Somerleyton Estate at the time. We had two children, a daughter, Linda, and a son Graham, who lives in New Zealand.

Right to Left – Marjorie with sister Myrtle

Joan Cudmore, (née Saunders), was an only child, age thirteen, when she was evacuated to Worksop with the Lowestoft Secondary School in June 1940.

A FEELING THAT I SHALL NEVER FORGET

Joan

I was in the lower years of Lowestoft Secondary School, which was a grammar school, when evacuation took place.

The journey was very traumatic. To add to that, there was a heat-wave and we girls had to wear thick fawn, lisle, cotton stockings. Our host village, Worksop, was excruciatingly hot and sticky but fortunately the next day, when we went to school, the edict went forth that we could wear ankle socks which was very much appreciated.

For most of us this was the furthest we had ever travelled from home. I remember the very large hall we were taken into when we arrived. The 'would be' foster parents were all lined up on one side, we were all lined up on the other, and they just picked us at random. We stood around very apprehensively and wondered who would claim us. This was very disconcerting and waiting in the village hall I developed a feeling that I shall never, ever, forget. I was an only child and I had never been away from home before. I didn't really have any close friends. I was a bit of a loner.

Eventually, two of us were chosen for billets two doors apart from each other. The foster parent of the other girl Hilda Noller, sensing that we might be upset that first night, suggested that I share the other girl's bedroom just for that occasion. This was agreed, and I believe we both silently wept ourselves to sleep, as I imagine many others did that first night.

My foster parents were a family called Overend. Mr Overend either owned or was in charge of a pharmacy at the top of the town. It was a lovely house with wall to wall carpeting which I had never seen before. This was a big contrast as I was used to a terrace house in May Road, Lowestoft.

When Sheffield, some twenty miles away, had air-raids we used to be able to see planes circling in the distance. I had to move after about six months because the lady's mother lived in Sheffield and she was alone. They decided she should come back to Worksop as it was deemed a lot safer. That meant I had to go.

I moved to the Lockwood's and that was a lovely house too. Mrs Lockwood was a retired teacher and he was a salesman. Not a door to door salesman, he went factory to factory. He was based in Sheffield at one of the stainless steel factories presumably one which had not been taken over for munitions. They had two sons in the army, one of them in India in the Punjab. They also had a daughter living at home. She was in her upper twenties.

When I got to this second billet I had a friend, Dorothy DeCaux, who was billeted just down the road from me. I often used to be sorting out my bicycle, which I had by that time acquired, and she used to walk past. She really 'adopted' me and we kept in touch until she died. She was the only close friend I had at school. She married a farmer, became Dorothy Youngs, and lived at Muckle Hill Farm near North Walsham.

We were on half-time education at the local school. This meant that on alternate weeks the local children went in the morning and we went in the afternoon. The worst thing was carrying everything. The local children had their desks and lockers full, so everything we needed we had to carry back and forth with us; cookery equipment, PT kits, craft things and text books.

I think the Lowestoft Secondary School was one of the few schools that had all their children in one town. A lot of the schools were split up, part in one town and part in another. Perhaps it was because we were a grammar school and therefore our teachers taught specific subjects. The first two years we had Miss Holland who travelled with us from Lowestoft. I also remember Mr Neal, Miss Joels, and Miss Walsh the PE teacher. Many of the younger male teachers had been called up. When we got to the fourth and fifth forms we sometimes had lectures in another building near the school. There was only six of us in the sixth form and I remember going to Whitwell to have our photograph taken. We went to the Girl Guides at the Priory which was fairly near the school in Worksop.

My father was in the grocery trade and worked at Devereux's shop in North Lowestoft. My parents visited me once and found out how lucky I was with my billets. My cousin, was evacuated to Glossop. As my mother and father were coming to visit me, her parents asked my parents to go and visit her. They found that she was sleeping in the bed next to the wife and on the other side of the wife was the husband! So, she was then moved. One of my mother's friend's daughter was sleeping with the wife in the bed during the night time, and the miner who was on night shift, slept in the same bed in the day time. So she was also moved. The allowance paid to the host families for taking the evacuee children was quite generous, so some families tried to squeeze in another child. It was lucky that I had an aunt in Spilsby in Lincolnshire where my mother could go and stay. This meant I would also go and stay when my mother was there.

I remember how we dreaded the end of each assembly because at the end Mr Brooks, the Headmaster, would come in and call out names. The odds were that if he called yours, it wasn't good news. Sometimes it was because families had been killed in air-raids back home. We were always glad when we got out of assembly without our name being called.

The older school children in Worksop always had a week off in October to go potato picking, so we did the same. We followed the machines along the field, picked up the potatoes, filled up a double sack, and every now and then emptied it into a vehicle that followed. We were paid a few pence for this. We did all sorts of things at the weekends tennis; concerts, craftwork, and hockey. In the summer holidays we cycled. I had no gears on my bicycle but we still went youth hostelling at Derwent and cycled over to Sheffield, about twenty miles away, to hear the Hallé Orchestra.

Some holidays I managed to get back home, dodging the bombs. I did the school certificate with matriculation and I was always going to be a language teacher because languages fascinated me. But after two terms in the sixth form at Worksop, where it seemed an anti-climax with only six of us there, three gentlemen came from the Inland Revenue in Lowestoft. They were desperate for people to employ as so many had been 'called up'. So, three of us were lured back leaving the sixth form to join the Inspector of Taxes Office in Lowestoft which was near the Grand Hotel. It was a great surprise to my parents who had bought me a new school blazer only the week before. They didn't mind in the least as they were glad to have me back. I didn't realise how awful it was for my parents to send me away until I had children of my own. I had been in Worksop for three years.

We were told the positions were only temporary and for nearly two years we filed everything numerical and alphabetically and I nearly went mad. As soon as the war finished there was the first reconstruction exam, and then you became established. I stayed for four and a half years until I got married.

During the war, my parents' house in May Road, Lowestoft was bombed. When I came back after the war we lived on a piece of ground that my grandmother owned which had two railway carriages on it. So we lived there in converted railway carriages until a house was ready for us which was not until after peace was declared.

I met my late husband, Charles, at Boston Lodge Youth Club in Lowestoft. During the war he was evacuated to a farm in Garboldisham and went to the village school there which consisted of one room with a curtain drawn across the middle. On one side was 5-12 year olds and the other side were the older ones. There was only one teacher. He was there until he was fifteen living on a friend's farm. He was an evacuee for only six months, coming back when he was old enough to make his own decision. He went into teaching being part of the emergency teacher programme at the end of the war and was trained at Wymondham College. My husband and I were involved with the Lowestoft and District Talking Newspaper for the Blind and also for the blind, the Three Rivers for Beccles, Bungay and Halesworth.

We went back to Worksop once in the 1950s and stayed with my second foster mother and her husband. My husband and I attended some of the reunions, the big ones, fifty, sixty, and seventy years.

Joan on the right with her foster mother, Mrs Lockwood

Ivan Barber was five years old and attending Lovewell Road School when he was evacuated from Lowestoft to Glossop in Derbyshire with his older sister, Kathleen, who was six. He had two brothers too young to be evacuated, Raymond and Alan, who stayed at home with their mother.

NO BEACH, OR SEA, IN GLOSSOP

Ivan on the left with sister Kathleen

It must have been heart-breaking for my mother to see my sister and I leave by coach for Lowestoft Railway station, knowing we would go with hundreds of other children by train to Glossop. We left Lowestoft at 9.55am and arrived at Glossop at 5.44pm, approximately an eight hour journey. All I can remember was the dark tunnel we went through and that I was frightened till we saw daylight again. I think it was the Woodhead Tunnel.

At Glossop, we walked down the hilly road to the market place where people were waiting to take evacuees in, but most didn't want to take two. Mother had told Kathleen, who was older than me, that we were not to be parted. So we were put on a bus, with other children, to travel round Glossop to find a billet that would take two. By this time, we were getting tired and my sister tells me that I was crying. We went up Whitfield Cross, turned left at the top, and that is where the bus stopped and we got out. Some people were talking, and a lady said, 'I'll have the little girl.' and then another lady, who turned out to be her neighbour, said, 'I'll have the little boy.'

I was with Mr and Mrs Winterbottom and Kathleen was next door. I slept the first night at my billet. However, Kathleen was very concerned about me, because mother had told her, 'You have got to watch Ivan.' Therefore, she insisted that the next night I went and slept with her at her foster parents' house. I did that for about four nights, to keep Kathleen happy, because she thought I might disappear.

Shortly after arriving, Kathleen asked her foster parents, Mr and Mrs Cartwright, where the beach was. She was shocked when she was told 'We have no beach, or sea, in Glossop.'

My foster parents lived in one of a row of cottages. They had no garden but had a small allotment opposite the house. I can remember going across the road in the morning to collect eggs from the chickens which they kept. In those days, food was rationed and everyone had ration books. We got the milk from a farm which was also across the road from our house. Milk was also delivered by a horse and small cart with milk churns on the back. Once I had a short ride in the back while out delivering milk with the farmer's wife. As we lived opposite the farm, we could see them taking the cows to the fields down the road. On one occasion, I was told I could go with them. I was walking behind them, when one decided to swish her tail right across my face!

Glossop is quite hilly and we enjoyed climbing up some of the hills. In wintertime, we had quite a lot of snow, and one of the neighbours of Mrs Winterbottom made me a sledge, which I enjoyed using on one of fields, after a snowfall.

We went to school in Glossop in a building they called 'Littlemoor'. We were with our Lowestoft classes, so we were happy. We lived next door to a chapel and I can remember going to the evening service. We went with our foster parents and I didn't mind too much because I knew Mr Winterbottom would be bringing sweets. The service did seem long at the time.

Glossop was safe from air attacks and bombing but I can remember the bright lights of Manchester, some fifteen miles away in the distance, and was told that Manchester was being bombed.

In Glossop, they had one cinema called The Empire, which we went to. It cost 3pence to sit in the back or 6pence at the front. Another memory I have is the worst flood on record at Glossop. There was thunder and lightning, and looking across the road, I could see water pouring off the wall onto the road. The next day, we found that houses had been flooded and machinery from the mill had been washed into the roads.

Another memory is of clogs. I would be sitting on the wall outside our house waiting for the people from the mill to walk past. At the time, it seemed to me you could hear the clogs they wore before you saw the people coming.

Eventually, our foster parents found a flat in Glossop for mum to come to and live in. So, we were able to move in with her and our young brothers, Raymond and Alan. Dad was away in the Merchant Navy but came to Glossop when on leave. I can remember, he once took us to Belle Vue Zoo in Manchester, where we had a ride on an elephant. That was great!

We stayed for five years and returned to Lowestoft in 1944, when the war was nearly over. When back home, I remember going to see my grandmother. When looking out of her window, I asked, 'What's that flying over the house?' Grandmother told me it was a 'doodle bug', which was really a flying bomb, with wings.

I married my wife Mary and we went back to Glossop twice after the war. I wish I had gone back earlier because, unfortunately, I had left it too late and my foster parents had died. I did my National Service and worked as an engineer for Zephyr Cams in Lowestoft. If I had been older when I was evacuated, I would have remembered more of my life in Glossop.

Iris Day (née Wilton), one of four siblings, was seven years old when she was evacuated from Roman Hill School in Lowestoft in June 1940 to Creswell in Derbyshire. This account was extracted from two stories written by Iris about her evacuation experience.

ONE OF THE LUCKY ONES

Iris on the right with Mrs May Cottrell and daughter Enid

The story of my evacuation begins at Lowestoft Railway Station. There were children from all different schools, myself from Roman Hill Junior. I was seven and a half, and my brother, Eric, ten years old. My two sisters were also on the station with their own classes.

Mothers with young babies were on the outside of the station trying to get a last glimpse of their children. We were bustled aboard the steam engine, which sent up clouds of murky smoke as we left the station. We strained our heads out of the windows for one last look, thinking this was to be just like a short holiday. Some children were crying, some sick and some had not been used to going away from home. My younger sister, Sheila, was just five years old and went to St. Andrews Infant School in Lowestoft. Her teacher looked after her on the train. My oldest sister, Violet, who was twelve years old and therefore went to Church Road School, went to Langwith with her school. I think my mother expected us all to be together.

I was in a carriage with my friend, Betty, other class friends, and our teacher. The scenery changed. Stone walls around the fields gave a very different look. What seemed like mountains to us were explained by the teacher, to be slag heaps from the pit. Buildings and huge chimneys blotted the horizon with massive bucket like objects going back and forth to the pit on overhead wires. It looked dark and dreary but exciting as we all clambered to the windows to watch.

At the train station were people with cars and bikes and also some buses. First we were taken to a building to have some refreshments. In my memory, it was the local Regor Cinema. We were given food and drink and had a check over then were taken to see where we would be living. I was to stay with an elderly couple a Mr and Mrs Cottrell and my friend Betty went a few doors away. After tea, I met Betty and we met other class mates on the green at the front of the houses. Someone brought my younger sister Sheila to see me, then took her back to bed as she was very tired. I still didn't know where my brother Eric was. He was unlucky and didn't have a very good foster home.

That night, I slept in a strange house, in a strange bed, in a bedroom of my own for the first time, in a village I had never heard of. It was the first time I had been by myself, I was homesick and hoped I wouldn't be there long. However, Grandma and Grandad Cottrell were very kind.

I changed foster parents and went over the road to May and Fred Cottrell's house. Fred was the son of the elderly Cottrells, who had not been able to cope, as they weren't well. I still ran errands for them and helped a bit. I came from a large family, so was quite used to doing and helping with washing up, etc. May and Fred had a daughter nearly a year younger than myself, Enid and I got on well.

I liked living with this foster family and I was extremely lucky to have a good foster mother, May, and foster father, Fred. Fred played the drums and some Saturday evenings would play in the band at dances.

Enid and I used to dance together, we thought we were very grown up. We spent a lot of time out walking and playing in Creswell Crags and exploring the caves, but most of them were boarded up.

May Cottrell was a very warm hard working lady. She worked at the pit canteen but still found time to sew dresses for Sunday school anniversaries and parties. She was also a good home maker. Once a week there was the smell of homemade bread and cakes if there were enough rations to spare. The only commodity that wasn't short was coal, as Fred had a regular load delivered. He didn't work down the pit but was on the top screens, as his eyesight and hearing were poor.

Saturday was the day to get in the food queue. We would all go down to the butchers to buy, if lucky, a pork pie, or sausages, or anything that was on offer. Sometimes we went on the bus to Clowne and managed to buy extra there, which we divided between the two grandmas, family and ourselves.

Once, American soldiers came to Creswell, during the school holidays. They used the cycle shed in the Infant School as a cook house. "Got any gum chum?" we used to say. They were very generous and gave us candy bars and we got the odd tin of Spam and dried egg. They were good to us children and we were sorry to see them leave.

I also went potato picking. We used to eat our sandwiches and slide down the haystack, which was under cover. The boys were the most daring and we used to go home tired out and dirty but with a bit more pocket money.

Mum was living at her sister's in Oldham, with my two youngest brothers. Dad was in the army. He came to Creswell, as Mum had a letter from May Cottrell telling her they had put my brother, Eric, in a hostel for unwanted children. Dad came over, went to the hostel, and against opposition from the staff, took Eric to live with Mum. Dad was furious that Eric had been treated like that.

I had a spell of about one month in the isolation hospital, as I had Scarlet Fever. So, a month before Christmas, I was at Marsden Moor, on the edge of the National Trust property. May Cottrell was my only visitor and used to talk to me through a window partition. Enid had to go into the isolation hospital when she had Diphtheria. When she went away, I came home from school to find some of the rooms taped off because they had to be fumigated.

We had a lovely summer and played at the Gripps and the Craggs. I loved school, came top in English and Maths, and was good at Art but in History I wasn't too keen. I wish I had been doing things like the children do now. The winters were white and wonderful but we didn't even have a half day off school because of it. I was one of the lucky ones, a good loving home, and friends, others have different tales to tell. Fred said he felt very proud when both Enid and I passed the scholarship in the same year. I couldn't take up my place at Lowestoft, until after the war, as my mother was still in Lancashire. So, I went to the Senior School in Creswell and we still had our own teacher, Mr Orchard, until we came back home.

I was sad to leave but at the same time looking forward to Lowestoft, going on the beach, resuming our old way of life and going to a new school. Although I had been to Lancashire when my dad had leave, it seemed strange to be back with a family. We were home for the celebrations of V. E. Day.

I have been back to Creswell on a number of occasions and kept in touch by letter and phone. We all led busy lives but loved visiting the old haunts and people. Sadly Fred Cottrell died whilst on holiday with May. Enid and her husband Barrie always have a warm welcome ready. They came down to Lowestoft to join in the 70th Anniversary of our evacuation 2010.

I married Ralph Day. Another evacuee, Margaret Taylor, married his brother Ronald. However, Margaret and I didn't know each other as evacuees although we were both in Creswell. We finally met several years later in a Lowestoft youth club, where we, in turn, met the Day brothers. We two evacuees, now related through these marriages, have remained friends ever since.

I stayed in Lowestoft all my life and worked as a secretary/receptionist in a medical practice. I was always an avid reader of books and I joined the U3A Writers group which suited me well as in addition to writing stories, I wrote a number of poems including the one which was read out at my foster mother, May Cottrell's funeral.

I attended many of the Lowestoft Evacuee Reunions and we went on several occasions by coach to Creswell and this allowed me to meet up with Enid once again. Evacuation changed my life, as it created a lifelong friendship with Enid by staying the war years at her home with the Cottrell family.

Margaret Day (née Taylor), went to Dell Road Primary School and was evacuated to Creswell in Derbyshire. Margaret was the youngest of four children. All her siblings were too old to be evacuated.

RATHER HAVE BEEN IN HOSPITAL

Margaret

I was eight and a half when I was evacuated. Three and a half thousand children left Lowestoft that day. There was another girl of my age, who lived two doors away from me, and our mothers told us to try and keep together, which we did.

Unfortunately we didn't have a very good billet so I don't like to talk about it. Although it wasn't very nice, at least, we girls were together and had each other. The man at the billet worked in the pit which I think most did. They had a son and daughter of their own. To be honest, today they wouldn't have been allowed to take us. There was no bedroom for us, not even one to share; we slept on a mattress downstairs.

Because there was so many children we could only go to school four mornings a week. We had lovely trips out with the school. I have a photograph of Sherwood Forest and The Crags at Creswell. The Crags are a tourist attraction now and the caves are barred up, however, we used to run in and out of them at that time. On one of our trips we went to the coal mine and went down in the cage into the pit. Well, that wouldn't be allowed today.

I was quite happy in school. We had our own teachers from Lowestoft with us. One of our teachers, Miss Hogg, stayed there and became headmistress of that school. Miss Capps also came with us.

While I was in Creswell I caught scarlet fever and went into hospital. People were not allowed to visit me. While I was in there a bomb dropped. I can remember it very well. I think that was about the only bomb that dropped on Creswell. I was in the hospital for about four weeks and I thought it was wonderful because I was well looked after in there. I would have rather been in hospital than be back in the billet.

My mum couldn't come to see me at first, nor my friend's mother. The war still being on made it difficult. When she eventually did come and saw how things were, she decided, on the spot, to take me home and I went back with her. My friend also returned home shortly afterwards.

When I got home Dell Road School was still closed because it was being use as a billet for soldiers. Therefore, I went to Gorleston Road School for about a year.

The war was still on and we had some really bad air raids. I was playing with one of my cousins, who had also come back home. She lived opposite us in Sycamore Avenue. My aunt told me to run home because the siren was going. I ran from her house, over the road, and through a passage way. I got halfway through the passageway and there was a bang. I can remember being terrified and screaming for my mum. She came running towards me and took me down the dugout in the garden.

My older brother, Harold, was killed in the war. He was in the army, but he was killed on board a boat travelling from Africa to Italy. The boat was hit by a bomb. The bomb exploded but the boat didn't sink. Someone came to see my mum after the war and said he was killed by the blast but that there was not a mark on him. What upset my mum a great deal, was that he hated the sea. You wouldn't even get him on the beach. But because they were going into battle at Monti Casino they buried him at sea. Therefore he doesn't have a war gave, as such, but his name is on the plaque at Monti Casino.

My dad was in the First World War so he didn't go in the army but he was in the Home Guard clearing all the rubble away after the bombings. My sister, who was ten years older than me, worked at the War Office and was billeted in Windsor. Lord Louis Mountbatten was her boss.

I'm pleased to say that in June 2019 my son, David, made one of my bucket list wishes come true. He announced that he was taking me to see the World War Two evacuees' memorial statue recently installed at the National Memorial Arboretum in Litchfield, Staffordshire. It was commissioned by the British Evacuee Association and designed by well-known sculptor Morris Blik and unveiled in July 2017. It is inscribed with the words 'Every Which Way'. It was a wonderful day and it will stay in my memory forever.

Margaret visiting National Memorial Arboretum in 2018

Keith Bellward was one of three brothers evacuated from Lowestoft to Glossop in June 1940. Keith was the eldest, Eric was in the middle, and Steve was the youngest.

WE PLAYED UP AND HOWLED A BIT

Keith on the right with brothers Eric and Steve

We were living in Wellington Esplanade and I was at Lovewell Road School aged seven, when my two younger brothers Eric and Steve and I went to Glossop. We left on 3rd June and I turned eight on 10th June. I can't remember that birthday, things were different away from our parents. The bus that picked us up from school and took us to the railway station was a double-decked corporation bus, chocolate, and cream.

When we got to Glossop, we were taken to the Victoria Hall and given tea and food. Then people from Glossop and the surrounding district came and picked out who they wanted. Unfortunately, at the end of the day there was still several of us left. So the billeting officer, Mr Blackman, took me, my two brothers and a boy called Keith, with him to find us billets. They found Keith a billet before they found one for us. They eventually found one but the lady could only take two. We played up and howled a bit but they said there was nothing they could do. So my brother, Eric, went to a different billet from Steve and me. Steve, being the youngest, stayed with me because my mother had told me to look after him.

When I got to Glossop I went to the Duke of Norfolk School. There were minor spats between us and the local boys because we were 'foreigners' and spoke differently but generally we mixed in fairly well. We took a lot of our own teachers with us. Mrs Hardingham, Miss Hook, Mr Outlaw, and Mrs McKendra. While I was there I did a paper round. Sometimes, people would complain the paper was late. That was because I was standing at the bottom of the garden reading it! I was in three different billets.

FIRST BILLET

Steve and I were billeted with Mrs Wardle in Manor Park Road. Eric was billeted in Silk Street with Miss Fisher.

Mrs Wardle had two other people living there. One was a lodger named Mr Simpson. I think he was a gang man on the roads. I should imagine he had a three month contract, then would move on to wherever they were going next. The other person was a boy evacuee from Manchester called Mathew. Mrs Wardle was an old lady in her seventies. It must have been difficult for her to have three young boys to look after. We three boys were in one room. There was a double bed which me and my brother had and Mathew was in the single bed. We never went hungry but there wasn't much food available during the war. We were never ill-treated but we did have to do work like sweep up. However, I think that was a good thing.

There were no food parcels from home because mother couldn't afford it. I'm the eldest of sixteen children, eight boys and eight girls, all still alive except for one sister, Molly. I have a sister in Australia and a sister in Portsmouth, the others are all around Lowestoft.

I was with Mrs Wardle for about nine months. I don't know the reason why we were moved.

SECOND BILLET

We were moved to Mrs Woods in Victory Street. They were a mother and daughter. It was close to a basket maker's named Mayes. That house has now been demolished. I don't remember much about this billet but, again, we were there for about nine months.

THIRD BILLET

All of a sudden we moved again to Mr and Mrs Mottram in George Street. I remember when we were at George Street there were two other evacuees staying on the corner of Manor Park Road at the pub called the Commercial Inn. They were Jo and Terry. We didn't know each other beforehand even though we were at the same school in Lowestoft.

My brother, Eric, was very lucky because the lady he was with had quite a bit of money and she brought him home to Lowestoft once for about a week. She also took him to Cadburys at Birmingham so he fared a lot better. He remained in the same billet for all of the war. My younger brother Steve and I were together all the time. I felt a bit hard done by at the time when we were disciplined. However, when you get older you realise you need to correct children. They were only doing the right thing.

We were away five years almost to the day. My father was in the fire service and he came up to see us once but I never saw my mother perhaps because of all the children she had to look after.

My brothers came back at the same time as me. When we were told we were going back home I was a bit apprehensive. When you are taken away that young, and for that period of time, you don't remember what you are going back to. Mother had more children and had moved on to another house which was quite crowded. I felt a bit like a stranger in that house.

It was soon July and the schools broke up. Therefore I went to Notley Road School for only about three weeks. I then went straight out to work for George Reeve's Dairy in Stradbroke Road, Pakefield.

I have been back to Glossop twenty-five or thirty times. The first time was in 1949. Mrs Wardle from the first billet and Miss Fisher who Eric had been billeted with had passed away.

When I first went back, we stayed with Mrs Mottram, from my third billet, on about three occasions. When she got too old, we stayed with her daughter. I am still in touch with Mrs Mottram's grandchildren. My wife, Jean, and I used to motor up but these last few times I have gone on the trips organised by the Lowestoft Evacuee Society. My brothers never went back or attended any reunions.

Foster parents Mr and Mrs Mottram

Mary Draper (née James) was five years old when she was evacuated to Barlborough near Chesterfield in Derbyshire in June 1940. Her three year old sister, Violet, went with her.

THE WAR DID US A FAVOUR

Mary on the right with sister Violet

We were two little girls, Mary and Violet James. When we were aged three and one and a half, our mother took us to Oulton Broad railway station and put us in the waiting room. The train must have come in. She went out of the waiting room and must have got on the train going to Norwich. We never saw her again. I had spent a lot of time with my auntie and knew where she lived, so I took my sister's hand and we walked to her house. From then we lived with Dad with the help of his sister, our Auntie Mary.

I started Gorleston Road School at Easter when I was five. It was in the following June that we were evacuated. Our Dad was a good dad. He was forty-six years old and had been in the army for twenty one years. He was then going into the Home Guard.

We were aged five and three respectively, when we were evacuated. Violet was not old enough to go, but Dad got special permission for her to come with me because we didn't have a mother. We weren't told that we were going anywhere. We were just put on a bus, then put on a train and away we went. Violet came with me on condition that we wouldn't be parted. We can't remember the train journey to Barlborough near Chesterfield but my late husband, Owen, who was at the same school and ten and a half years old, later told me he looked after me and Violet. He walked up and down the train with violet in his arms as she cried all the way.

In a hall at Barlborough, the people who were providing billets were picking children out. A lot of the children had already been chosen when we went with Mr and Mrs Bacon. Mr Bacon had left off late from work and therefore they got to the hall late. Mrs Bacon had previously said they would take one little boy but when she saw us she said to Mr Bacon, 'I'm going to take them home and love them.' This she did till the day she died. So that was it, they were our foster parents and they became Uncle Bob and Auntie Bee to us. It was lovely for us to have a mum and we were the children they never had. We were their family, their girls. We had six years of happiness and those years were the best of our childhood. We had no toys with us as we had taken only the bare necessities. I still have the towel I was given to take with me. Auntie Bee kept both our towels and gave them to us later. Violet also has hers. I still have the book I was given for good attendance at Sunday school.

The school didn't like evacuees. When we had exams we were told not to turn our head; well one day I did. I was caned ten times on each hand and when I got home my hands were swollen. After Uncle and Auntie saw my hands Uncle went to the school. 'Don't you take things out on my two girls,' he said, and threatened to 'go to the top'. The next day when I went to school I had to sit in the 'Baby Chair'!

I got scarlet fever and was in hospital. Auntie used to come every day and talk to me standing on a platform outside the window because she wasn't allowed in. I had a cold sore on my lip and it wouldn't get better, which meant I wasn't allowed home. The nurse sat with me one night to see if I was touching it. I didn't touch it during the day but I was touching it in my sleep. The nurse tied some books to my arms so I couldn't lift them to touch it. After that, it went away and I was able to go home.

We saw Dad once a year. He came on Easter Saturday and went home Easter Monday. If anything had happened to Dad, Auntie and Uncle would have adopted us.

After the war Dad wanted us home. It was awful for us and for Auntie and Uncle. It took us all a long time to get over it. The day we came home to Lowestoft we went to our Auntie Mary's. Violet ran upstairs and locked herself in the bedroom and wouldn't come out. She wanted to go 'home' to Derbyshire. Coming back to Lowestoft again was far worse than being evacuated.

Dad died when Violet was sixteen and I was eighteen. Violet went back to live with Auntie and Uncle in Derbyshire. I was already engaged, to Owen, so I stayed in Lowestoft. If I hadn't met Owen I would also have also gone back.

When she went back to Derbyshire to live, Violet met Ken, who was from Brimington. They married and she stayed there. I stayed in Lowestoft and married Owen. It was upsetting to be parted from Violet but I went back 'home' to Derbyshire every year with my family. It will always be home to me. Violet looked after both Auntie and Uncle till the day they died.

Margaret Ellis, (née Durrell), went to Lovewell Road School and was about six years old when she was evacuated from Lowestoft to Glossop in June 1940. She had a baby brother, James born at the beginning of the war in 1939, who stayed at home.

AUNT ETHEL TOOK ME EVERYWHERE

Margaret

My mother always said I ran away *to* school. The playground of Lovewell Road School was opposite our house and I went in with the other children one day and they let me stay!

I didn't go by train with the other children when they were evacuated. I don't know why, but I stayed at home even though I was old enough to go. However, the air-raids frightened me and in the end, I would refuse to come out of the air-raid shelter. My parents then realised that I, also, needed to be evacuated. My father was in the Fire Service. He later said that bombs went down on Kirkley Fen, close to our house, and didn't explode.

Mrs Youngman, who lived two doors from us along Beaconsfield Road, had two sons Brian and Alan. They were already in Glossop, in Mount Street with Mrs Fox. When Mrs Youngman went to Glossop to visit her boys she found me accommodation in the same road. I then went to Glossop by train with her.

My foster parents were Mr and Mrs Hall and I called them Uncle Harry and Auntie Frances. Mrs Hall's sister, who worked at the cotton mill, lived with them and I called her Auntie Ethel. I was all on my own and very anxious. When I went into the house they were all sitting there. Auntie Frances said, 'Are you going to kiss Uncle Harry?' I said no! He was sitting in his chair, very formal, a civil servant in a pinstriped suit. He was nothing like my dad who was a rugged man, so I wouldn't kiss him. Mr Hall was a churchwarden at Whitfield Church and when he went to the pub they used to call him 'Mr Harry'.

When I was first there, I remember crying in bed and counting things on the wallpaper. They didn't like me sucking my thumb so I used to try and keep it in my nightie so that I wouldn't. However, I was lucky, it was a comfortable home and I got on very well with Mrs Hall and her sister Ethel. Some children had awful billets.

Mrs Hall had another sister, Amy, who was Head Cook for the Bishop of Manchester, Dr Guy Warman. His wife gave me a toby jug, 'Old Mother Gamp'. I still have it today.

I spent most of the time with Aunt Ethel the sister of my foster mother. She was the one who looked after me and took me out and about. They didn't have any family of their own and they looked after me well. In fact I was 'ruined'.

I went to Littlemore School, Mr East was the Headmaster. I still see some of the children who went to Littlemore School even now. I also went to Whitfield Church of England School. I had a friend while I was there, Sheila. She was an evacuee from Lowestoft but I didn't know her before I went to Glossop. The foster parents who she was billeted with adopted her. She stayed there and then eventually immigrated to Canada. She was my best friend in Glossop. We were also friends with Ronnie Kinder who was the telegram boy.

It was hard work for my mother bringing up my young brother during the war, what with all the blackouts. She came to visit me and brought my brother with her. On the train the military helped her with him and her suitcases. My father only came to visit me once because he didn't get paid holiday and therefore they couldn't afford it. On the occasion that he did come, he said to my mother, 'Thank goodness, Mother, there will be no air-raid warning tonight.' The air-raid warning went off in Glossop and he couldn't believe it.

I didn't have any feelings about coming home. We knew we would come back and we just did as we were told. My brother was born in June 1939 and my mother lavished everything on him. I took the attitude that he was lucky to stay at home with mother, while I was sent away. I told my mum that she didn't want me. I think now that it was a horrible thing to say.

After I came back home, I received some letters from Ronnie Kinder, the telegram boy. When I went to Glossop after the war, I thought I would go and see Ronnie. However, the Post Office wasn't there anymore. Nobody in Mount Street knew him either. I wrote to the local paper and a friend of his saw the letter. He told Ronnie, who wrote back. I still get a card every Christmas from Ronnie. He became the Post Master at Glossop. He is the only person I know in Glossop now.

I passed the scholarship while I was in Glossop. When I came home I went back to Lovewell Road School for a while and then Lowestoft Grammar School. I didn't like it at the Grammar School. I left and got a job in the office at the railway station where I met my husband, Sid. He was invalided out of his National Service and became a shunter then a Guard and finally a porter in Lowestoft station.

Sadly, Aunt Ethel died in 1943 while I was still in Glossop. For me, as a child, she just seemed to disappear from my life. Aunt Ethel was very important to me, she looked after me well. Eventually I found out where her grave is and went back to visit her there.

After the war, Uncle Harry and Auntie Frances came to Lowestoft, to ours, for holidays. They also attended my wedding to Sidney at St John's Church. When Uncle Harry retired, they moved to Lowestoft and bought a house close to me. Aunt Frances died in 1968 and I didn't see so much of Uncle Harry after that.

On a recent visit back to Glossop, I went to Whitfield Church where I rang the bells on VE day and I was able to ring the bells again.

My going to Glossop not only had a big influence on my life, but on my foster parents lives too.

My foster mother's sister, Aunt Ethel

Brian Baxter was 6 years old and attending Lovewell Road Infants School, Lowestoft when he was evacuated to Glossop in Derbyshire on Sunday 2nd June 1940. He then moved on to Whitwell, Derbyshire to be with his sisters Edna, and Ruby.

MACHINE GUNNED BY A GERMAN FIGHTER PLANE

Brian, middle row, third from the right

I have very little memory, of leaving Lowestoft by train as an evacuee. I was, as far as I can recollect, an infant at Lovewell Road School. Our family lived in Notley Road, South Lowestoft. I was the youngest of five and the only boy. Throughout my schooling, I was at Lovewell Road and Notley Road Schools.

During the war, my second youngest sister, Muriel, was in service at Major Warwick's house in Nottingham. I believe I went there one day, with my mother, to see her. My oldest sister, Margaret, stayed in Lowestoft.

I can vaguely remember being picked out, upon arrival at Glossop. I can remember an air raid whilst I was there. Another big event that sticks in my mind is of spilling a tin of paint. I became very ill while I was living at this billet and my father came to see me. Whatever happened, I was moved to Whitwell, to be with my sisters Edna and Ruby. Thus, the first chapter of my early days as an evacuee, ended.

My two sisters had been taken in by a family called Webster, who lived in Hanger Hill which I believe is now Foxes Road. That is where I joined them from Glossop. I believe my second eldest sister, Edna, worked in Worksop. She had to cycle there every day a distance of about five miles each way.

I am fairly sure that the Websters had, at least, two daughters. Mr Webster was a keen woodsman. What his occupation was I don't know. He kept in his shed; a number of ferrets. I seem to recall that, the lady next door lived on her own and had evacuees as well. I can remember my sister, Ruby, serving milk from a milk churn, with a ladle, directly into milk jugs. This was from the back of a pony and trap. I was very much happier at Whitwell. I had a very good friend there, who lived directly opposite the school, a local boy Kenny Allen.

Upon the arrival of my mother and father in Whitwell, we moved as a family to live with the Wilds, at 86, Portland Street. They had three sons, Eric, Dennis and John, (Juddy), I believe. A stream ran very close to the house and I spent many great hours playing in the water with friends. We used to build small boats and race them down the stream. Whilst there, I did potato picking and planting and other jobs on the farm.

I can remember that we had some great sledging days when the snow came. My father worked at Steetley Quarry and drove a huge digger, mining great slabs of stone for runways, I understand.

My dad did serve in the First World War and was so keen to be involved that he enlisted when he was just fourteen years old, whilst the minimum age officially allowed was eighteen. Some years later, he laid claim to being the youngest person on the British side in that war. As I understand it, this claim was challenged by a man living in Australia – I must admit I never knew the outcome.

We came back home to Lowestoft during the latter part of the war, when the doodle bugs were coming over. We used to wait for the engine to cut out, then the crash. It was, either the air raid shelter, or under the stairs, when this happened. I am sure a barrage balloon was situated on Notley Road School playing field. Bombs fell in Notley Road and we were machine gunned by a fighter on one occasion. My first vivid memory of after the war, was of all the shops and streets suddenly being lit up when the black out shutters were taken down.

In 1955, when life settled down again after the war, I married a Lowestoft girl, Sheila, in St. Margaret's Church Lowestoft. We had two sons, Gary and Christopher, who now both live in East Anglia.

We eventually settled in Norwich, where I worked for Eastern Counties Newspapers for most of my life – first on the commercial side and then, eventually became Manager of the branches throughout East Anglia

Revisiting Whitwell After the War

The Lowestoft Evacuees Reunion Association was founded in 1990 by Christopher Brooks, a retired teacher. I joined this group in the mid 1990s and each year reunions were held in the Stella Morris church hall in Lowestoft.

In addition, coach trips were arranged to revisit the villages where we had been billeted. In my case Whitwell. Three of these trips are now described:

2007

On our reunion visit in 2007, I got off the coach at Whitwell and visited my old school, now the Community Centre, and met up with the management team, who suggested I come back in the afternoon and meet some pensioners, as they might know me. This, I duly did, and in the course of conversation, one of them said that they knew Kenny Allen the friend I had, when I was in Whitwell. I gave them my card and the following evening Kenny phoned me. His brother, who was born after the war, for some time ran a tea stall at the Jetty in Great Yarmouth, but has now moved to Somerset.

2008

The visit to Derbyshire on July 4th 2008, held particular significance for me, when, after a number of telephone conversations and nearly Seventy years apart, I finally met with Ken. He lives in retirement, just outside Whitwell, where we first met as youngsters. My wife, Sheila, was with me when we greeted Ken on the arrival of our coach in Whitwell. It was absolutely fantastic to meet again, after such a time span, and to reminisce.

2010

On our 2010 re-union in Clowne, I was fortunate to meet up with Iris and Ken Gray, who still live in Whitwell. Iris was one of the two sisters we first stayed with when we were evacuated. Kenny Allen, since we met up in 2008, had done some checking and had found Iris. We exchanged details, over the phone, and arranged to meet the next time we came to Clowne. So, there we were, Ken, Iris and me together again, for the first time, since the early forties. It was a wonderful get together.

Even when the activities of the Evacuee Association reduced, I still kept in touch with my good friend Kenny Allen who has sadly now passed away. We spoke every few months on the phone and exchanged Christmas cards – knowing Kenny, turned out to be a positive outcome of my evacuation, as he became a lifelong friend.

One further chapter in my life was Rotary and I was appointed Grand Master for the whole of the East Anglia region in 1995, a one year term. I remain a member of the Lowestoft branch right up to the present day.

Brenda Goldspink, (née Taylor), was seven years old and attending Church Road Infants School when she was evacuated from Lowestoft to Scarcliffe and later Clowne in Derbyshire. She had a younger brother, Peter, who stayed at home. Brenda kindly shared her own written story.

MY EVACUEE AND WARTIME EXPERIENCE

Brenda with her mother and brother Peter

I parted company with my mother on Lowestoft Railway Station, my gasmask case strapped over my shoulder. On arrival at a hall in Scarcliffe packed with adults and school children, our names were called out and we were delegated to families. I remained towards the last along with my two friends from school, twins Beryl and Rex. They lived at the top of Ipswich Road and I lived towards the bottom of Oxford Road, with a back alleyway between us. This area suffered extensive bomb damage during the war. Houses at the top of Ipswich Road in Lowestoft took direct hits, causing loss of life and were demolished. I remember a lovely young women being killed. This deeply saddened me.

As Beryl and Rex left the hall with their host family, I remember feeling very sad. I had assumed I would be with them. Another lady took me. They were staying on a farm and I was a long way from them up a lane and across the road. Thankfully, I was able to spend time on the farm with them, the farmer and his wife. When there, I was happy. I remember fondly being sat up upon a huge horse by the farmer and given a ride. I was so happy to be welcomed into this warm and friendly home.

However, my time spent in the billet up the lane was not a happy one. Upon my arrival, when taken up to my bedroom I recall vividly; a striped mattress; the lady present; feeling homesick and crying for my Mummy.

The property next to the house where I stayed was a bungalow. Between the gardens was a wooden criss-crossed fence, which I could see through. There, I would be able to talk to a lovely kind lady next door, which was comforting. When seeing and smelling French marigolds, I recall seeing a bed of them on the other side of that fence. Through this lady my parents would have been informed of my unhappiness while staying in that house.

A happy event was me being taken in a pony and trap with the twins, by the farmer, through the village to the fields, where the workers were harvesting the crops. Whilst travelling en-route I was surprised to see, walking along the road towards us, a familiar face. None other than my very young Auntie Venita (only three years and two months older than me). I can still see her now, with her upturned brimmed hat. She climbed on board the buggy with us to the fields of hay. How she got to Scarcliffe and back I have no idea.

My mother, along with my younger brother, Peter, travelled to be with me in order to re-home me. The day they arrived in Scarcliffe, my memory is of walking by myself along a lane to meet them. On both sides there were hedgerows, decked with tall purple weeds amidst cow parsley. When seen today, it reminds me so much of that occasion. I also remember my brother holding my mother's hand, walking towards me, and me feeling somewhat shy and overwhelmed.

Once more as a family, (apart from my Dad who remained in Lowestoft working on the docks) we lodged with a little old lady we called Granny Blacknell. She was so tiny. She wore long dark clothing, covered by an apron and a frilly cap on her head. On her tiny feet she wore black buttoned boots. Her cottage was dark and small with flag stone flooring and small windows. The outside toilet was quite a distance away from the cottage. Dry of course, with a hole cut into the plank of wood you sat upon. Newspapers were cut up, threaded on string, and hung up for toilet paper. The black print of newspapers rubbed off on the skin and one cannot help but imagine the result of this! The smell I can still recall. More farmyard, than sweet lavender! The toilet hut was situated amongst many fruit trees. I remember hearing the alarming news that a parachute had come down not far away. Was the person who came down with it hiding amongst those trees?

I have no idea how long we stayed in Scarcliffe. However, we came home, I imagine, because the air raids had eased. I recall hearing about a dreadful scare my father encountered whilst working on the deck of a ship in the harbour. A motor torpedo boat, probably. A bomb had landed on the deck, but miraculously didn't explode.

We remained back home until the situation became too dangerous to stay, with Doodle Bugs constantly landing on Lowestoft. The sound was terrible and the fire which expelled from the back of them was scary to watch. We would dash down into the Anderson Shelter, knowing, that when the drone of the engine ceased, a terrific bang would follow. One crashed down close to our house. Also, a huge (1,000 lb) bomb landed, leaving a massive crater in the middle of the alleyway linking Ipswich Road and Oxford Road.

Etched clearly in my memory, is being sent on an errand to the shop down the bottom of the road. I heard a loud roar of vehicles coming, carrying troops. Then from the sky, which had very low grey cloud, came veering straight down; a German Aircraft, followed by a second one. The pilots in their leather helmets and thick goggles were a scary sight. I dashed into a front garden and laid flat on the ground, underneath a concrete window sill. (I'd been told at school, to take cover this way) The soldiers in the moving vehicles shouted at me 'get down, get down'. All this time the pilots were firing tracer bullets which sparked flashing lights when pinging along the pavement. There had been no-air raid warning, due to the low cloud. This allowed enemy aircraft to fly under the radar. My poor mother, when hearing all the commotion, must have had her heart stop! She felt terrible that she had sent me down to the shop. As there was no air-raid warning, safety would have been taken for granted.

Many of us children used to play in the grounds of Adrian Lodge on Church Road, a large mansion like house with lots of grounds. The bomb that fell caused extensive damage. It was said, that the crater could have housed a double decker bus. Our house suffered from the blast. The windows and doors blew out and the ceilings came down. My Dad was in bed as he had to start work very early. The blast blew him up out of his bed, to the bedroom ceiling. The air was filled with acrid smoke. I remember seeing the bluey haze and all the dust through the entrance hatch of the shelter. As a result of this raid, off we had to go, back to Derbyshire. Destination Clowne.

At Clowne we lived as a family, my mum, brother, and myself, with a nice lady in a terraced house on the brow of a hill, on the Cresswell Road. At the bottom of the hill, lived my grandmother along with my Auntie Marjorie, her young son Keith, my young aunt Venita and Uncle Brian.

At the back of their house there was a lane with fields on the other side. This was our play area. We ran through one of the fields to where there was a stream. We would take a run and jump to the other side, often missing, which resulted in wet socks and shoes; sometimes much more! I used to enjoy cycling full pelt down the lane, but not so much pushing the cycle back up. Venita and I spent a lot of our time together. Not far off the road was a 'slag heap'. We would climb up to the top, find something suitable to sit upon and have great fun sliding down. We came off countless times, often dirtying our clothing and occasionally tearing them.

When spending time in the field where cows had been grazing, resulting in plenty of 'cow pats', I had the misfortune of treading slap bang into a 'fresh' one. I was wearing new shoes! On our many 'jaunts' we were scared to go home knowing, full well, we'd get a telling off! My time in Clowne was a much happier time, amongst many close family members.

After the war, when I was seventeen, I had a spell as a Radar Operator/Plotter in the Auxiliary Air Force. I then married and had two children. I have been to a number of evacuee reunions and trips to revisit our host villages. In 2018 I visited the National Arboretum Memorial in Shropshire commemorating evacuees.

Brenda on the left with Venita, her young aunt

Jean Gower (née Snowling), was ten years old when war broke out. She was an only child, living in St Peter's Street, Lowestoft and attending Church Road School. She was evacuated to Hillstown, Derbyshire. Jean has written her own story and shares it here.

MY OWN PARTICULAR WAR

Jean dressed as a sunflower

I was just a small child when the Second World War was declared. I had been listening for weeks to my parents discussing the inevitability of war and found the outlook frightening. My father joined the Home Guard. With air-raids happening with monotonous regularity, his night duty would include directing people, caught out on the streets, to the nearest shelters. These were narrow purpose-built underground tunnels with long wooden benches running along both sides. They were smelly, dark and dank.

From my bedroom window in Lowestoft, I could just see St. Margaret's church steeple, and on certain evenings I could hear the bells. They were silenced for the duration of the war and were only used as a warning in the event of an enemy invasion. To this day I dislike the sound of church bells. For me their melancholy chimes seem to herald a prelude of doom.

It was common knowledge that the schools were going to be evacuated. But there was a choice whether to send your children or not, and a few stayed behind. Some of the children that stayed behind ran wild for a couple of years because there was no schooling for them. All education was shot to pieces.

I was evacuated to a small place called Hillstown and was billeted with a friend, June, who I had grown up with. We had asked to be billeted together and a kind woman was willing to take the two of us in. I was not aware that they had picked us. It was all well organised and the billeting officers had lists of who we were and what we wanted. A lot of children didn't stay very long because they got homesick.

We were given to a couple in their fifties who had no children of their own. To simplify matters we were told to call them Aunt Fanny and Uncle Mark. They were very kind but strict and we had to do work. The man of the house was a miner and, of course, they had coal delivered to them as part of their wages. A huge lorry load of coal would be dumped outside the front gate, spreading over the pavement and blocking the road. So we would help shovel it into a wheel barrow and move it as quickly as possible. I used to clean the windows and sweep the floors. There were no vacuum cleaners in those days. We had to earn our keep, more or less.

Education was at a minimum. I recall our overworked teacher, Mr Bull, having just one classroom with several different age groups to cope with. He often asked us older ones, I was about 10 or 11, to take on a group of the younger ones and try to teach them.

We were later directed to attend one of the local schools. This was at a nearby town called Carr Vale about a mile from where most of the children were billeted. We walked there each day even in terrible weather. During the winter there was so much snow, the drifts reached to the top of fences measuring at least two metres high. We had to wade through deep falls of hard slush along the pavements in Wellington boots.

I didn't really mix with the local children much because I was with my friend and we were always together. If we mixed with anyone it was with the other evacuees. Aunt Fanny had a sister who lived in Sheffield. She had a son about our age. He used to come to the house and we would go to his.

June and I were acting silly one day. We were picking fluff off a blanket and Aunt Fanny came in and caught us. She was angry. We got into trouble for that and she made us write to our parents to tell them what we had done. However, it all blew over.

There was one air raid when we were there. A stray German plane came over and dropped a couple of bombs. They fell in a field and didn't do any damage. It was thought that they may have seen the moon shining on a water tower and expected to hit something important. That scared the life out of Aunt Fanny and Uncle Mark. They took us out of the bedroom and made us sleep in a cupboard under the stairs. It was dreadful. It was airless and full of polish and apples. It was an airless and claustrophobic cupboard.

There was an elderberry tree in the garden and Aunt Fanny, being a bit of a herbalist, picked the flowers, hung them up to dry until they turned brown, boiled them, strained them, and bottled the juice. She would give us a cupful every night declaring it was good for our health. I hated it! She also made elderberry syrup out of the berries which I found sickly but felt obliged to drink. The worst thing, though, was when she made liquorish and linseed tea. It smelt and tested like varnish and made me feel sick. There was one thing I enjoyed though, when the raspberries ripened in the garden, she would pick them, soak them in vinegar for three weeks, boil the liquid with lots of sugar, and bottle it. It was delicious on pancakes which we had every Monday for lunch.

Eventually, missing our families, we longed to go home. My friend left six months before I did. I then got lonely so I asked Mum if I could come home. I came back to Lowestoft in the middle of all the air-raids. Aunt Fanny made no bones about it when I left.

I shall never forget the sensation inside me as the train approached Lowestoft. After two years away from everything familiar, I suddenly had this terrible feeling of anti-climax. For a moment I wanted to return to the place that had become home to me. I realized there would be some sort of coming to terms with the people and relatives I hadn't seen for some time.

After quickly adapting, as children do, the next thing I had to get used to was being woken up several times during the night and hustled quickly outside to the air raid shelter in the garden. This became a common occurrence as most nights the loud wailing of the siren alerted everyone of an imminent air raid. There was the chug chug noise of the enemy aircraft overhead as they sought their target. Everyone wondered if it would be their turn next.

My mother was always very unconcerned though, she refused point blank to seek the questionable safety of the air-raid shelter. Instead, she would wander around the garden keeping an eye on the action informing us when the enemy planes had passed over. Then we would wait for the ear piercing scream of the falling bombs followed by an explosion somewhere. We would learn the next day of the destruction. One time a cousin of mine, Dora Aldred[1], was in a store in the main street which took a direct hit. She was blown to pieces, and just fourteen years old.

We learned to live together in some kind of harmony and would help each other when required. No one knew if they would see another tomorrow. That brought a feeling of affinity to bear. Food was short to non-existent like everything else. People learned to share. If mother managed to acquire something out of the ordinary, probably by queuing for long periods, we would have the young woman and her two children in from next door, to share. Even one small slice of Spam and a few mashed potatoes would be eaten with relative enjoyment.

The fish and chip shop, just along the road from where I lived in St Peter's street, opened when they were able to obtain supplies. On one occasion, at around six o'clock, my mother sent me to get chips for

---

[1] D E Aldred is listed as a civilian casualty of what is known as the 'Waller's Raid', which took place on 13th January 1942 ['The Air War Over Lowestoft 1939-1945', by Bob Collis and Simon Baker].

supper. In those days you could get a bagful for an old penny. It was a fine summer evening, all was quiet, and I stood waiting in anticipation of the treat ahead. The next thing, there was an excruciating ear-piercing whistle of bombs as they screamed through the air, then a terrific explosion. Glass from the windows came flying inwards and the ceiling caved in. I was lying beneath a heap of debris. I was on top of some people and beneath others. They, like me, had been waiting to be served. Eventually, we emerged from the chaos and I walked home with hardly a scratch, but minus the chips.

My mother, for once in her life, panicked and tried to get outside to see the damage for herself but my father prevented her, accepting it would be of little use. I will never forget her relief and joy when I walked through the door. I had been lucky.

There was a bit of a tie between me and my foster parents after the war. We wrote once or twice and they came to Lowestoft to visit us after I was married to a Lowestoft man, Reginald Gower, who was an engineer and tool maker. My husband and I went up to Derbyshire years later to visit them but Aunt Fanny had died. We had a car so took Uncle Mark to Sheffield to see his relatives.

I realize only too well that my own particular war was totally unremarkable, but there were those who paid the ultimate price, and it will be etched on my memory for all time.

Jean on the right

Melville Canham was six years old and attending Dell Road School, Lowestoft when he and his sister, Nancy, were evacuated to Creswell in Derbyshire in June 1940.

A LUCKY WAR

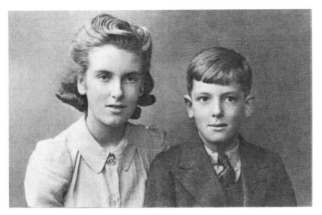
Melville on the right with sister Nancy

My sister Nancy and I were pupils at Dell Road School in 1940 when we were evacuated to Creswell. I was just over six years old and Nancy was nearly eleven. I have a photocopy of the letter which Nancy wrote home on our arrival. I reproduce the letter below exactly as it was written. ('Worksop' becomes 'Workshops' and 'charabancs' become 'charibans').

----

6 Dover Street
Creswell Workshops
Notts

Dear Darling Mummy and Daddy

I hope you are not upset about us for I have got into a very nice home, I am in no camp so there is nothing to worry about. When we arrived at Clown we were bustled out of the train and were put in to charibans and then of we went, after that we were put into a picture palace and the doctors looked at us and I was alright, then we had to sit down in

83

the seats and waited for our names to be called then my/our names was called (tho waiting a very long time to be called out.) I was sent out of the palace and a man say take these two but somebody said take them down to Mrs Wragg. A man took me and Melville arm-in-arm. We went across the road and there we saw a crowd of women. The man who we were with said (the next two words are illegible) and they all said bring them here and the man said come you here.

Mrs Wragg came and said come I will not separate you and so we were taken in. Mrs Wragg kissed us both and made us both at home. After her to little children came in and Mrs Wragg said I have to nice little children (of) mine (own). They were a little girl and a little boy the girl was 8 and the little boy 10 they are very nice little children and make you at home. So don't worry about us and I will not worry about you. But I have been very upset but am alright now so good by you will see the address. Come and see us soon won't you tell us when. Good by oh Cheerio   Mum + Dad

----

The last two lines are crowded in at the bottom of the page as she had obviously run out of space. There are also 14 Xs. I think these 'kisses' were written first and the final two lines inserted as an afterthought.

I have no recollection at all of the train and coach journey, but I clearly remember being in the cinema when we arrived. I was very excited as I thought we were going to see a picture, which was one of the greatest treats I knew. When no film materialised I was extremely disappointed.

My other memory of evacuation day is the bitter disappointment I felt at missing the very day on which the eggs under my father's hens were due to hatch, as I remembered how much I had enjoyed watching the chicks the year before. It surprises me how little I remember, like saying goodbye to Mum and Dad when we got on the train. But I was more concerned about the chicks. It just shows how children's minds work.

When we arrived Nancy and I were separated at first in the cinema. I think we must have been arranged by classes as our teachers would know who we were. I remember seeing Nancy making her way from the front to where I was at the back. I had thought she did this on her own initiative and thought 'oh I must collect Melville'. But from what I have read, the policy, I imagine, would have been to keep siblings together. In which case Nancy would have been told to find me. I had always believed that if Nancy had not made that effort we would have remained separated. At any rate I am very glad that I did not have to remain on my own as that would have made me very unhappy.

I also remember the crowd of women and how uncomfortable it was waiting for someone to 'claim' us. Of course we had to wait until someone would take two together. When we departed with Mrs Wragg we didn't have far to go as the house, in Dover Street, was opposite the cinema. Mrs Wragg had two children Doreen who was eight and Dennis who was ten. We got on quite well with them and were made to feel welcome.

I remember that as part of our first meal we had bananas and custard. It was the last time I saw bananas for a very long time as they disappeared from the shops. It must have been one of the last shipments after the fall of France. In fact I now eat a banana every day and every time I peel a banana I think how I would have loved to do this as a child.

In general I remember surprisingly little about my stay in Creswell. I recall the first day at school there, standing in the playground waiting for the door to this strange school to open. I can still see that door opening now. Other memories include playing at Creswell Crags where one summers day Mrs Wragg's little girl cut her foot very badly on a broken bottle as she was running about barefoot. I did, after all, get the chance to see films at the cinema, including one starring Shirley Temple.

We have a picture of me and Nancy and our mother in Creswell. In it I'm looking very upset and pouting, what my mother used to call 'sausage lips'. I expect it was because Mum was going away but it may have been some other very small thing. Mum used to say 'we don't want any sausage lips here'. I was quite good at 'sausage lips'.

We returned home after only a few months. Neither Nancy nor I could remember our return or when it took place, but I am sure it must have been before Christmas, which was so important to me when I was a child that I would certainly have remembered a Christmas spent away from home. The reason for our early return was that my mother could not settle without us and she spent a lot of time in Creswell to be with us. My father who continued his job as a railway signalman must have thought this was not a very good arrangement, and as the threat of invasion had passed and bombing in Lowestoft had not started, my parents thought it was safe for us to come home. During 1941 Nancy and I spent some months in the safety of an aunt's home in the village of Chignall near Chelmsford.

I have often thought that I am very glad that I wasn't an adult during the war. I think of what my parents must have been feeling when invasion was imminent. How would I have felt as a parent of a six year old child who had to go away and be evacuated?

I didn't really suffer because of the war. I mean we were bombed quite a bit when we got back to Lowestoft but Oulton Broad was very lucky. I lived in the Station House at Oulton Broad South near the bridge over the railway. There were no bombs within probably half a mile but Lowestoft was bombed heavily.

Nancy and I used to sleep in our Anderson Shelter in the garden. Mum and dad would stay in the house until the siren went then came down. This was because they knew that having to wake children up and get them out of the house during the night would be difficult, so we slept down there. I can remember lying on a bunk looking up at the official blue marks on the corrugated iron.

Strangely enough I don't think that I was as frightened then as I would be now because for a child there was a certain amount of excitement to it. As a child you didn't understand what would happen if a bomb did drop on you.

The Secondary school was evacuated to Worksop and they didn't come back till 1944. When I started at the Grammar school in 1945 most of the older children there had been away together and there was a bond between them; the children coming after them hadn't experienced what they had.

When we came back, apart from the time I attended the village school, I had a glorious year of not having to go to school. I was about seven then and I used to hope the war would go on until I was old enough not to ever go to school again.

They worry about children missing a day from school now but I missed an entire year of school and yet by 1945 I took the 11 plus and got to the grammar school and went on to Oxford. When we resumed school I couldn't even read properly.

I studied modern languages at Oxford University and after obtaining my degree I went on further to gain a Post Graduate Certificate of Education so I was qualified to teach. I then served three years in the RAF as an education officer, was married in 1959 and we had one son Julian. I went on to become librarian at the Lowestoft College, a position I held until I retired in 1999.

Evacuation didn't change the course of my life because I was there such a short time. I had a very lucky war really.

Melville after the war

Olive Guymer, (née Mummery), was thirteen when she was evacuated to Shirebrook, Derbyshire. She had two older brothers, Leonard and Victor, who were both in the forces. Olive's father was in the ARP (Air Raid Precautions) and her mother, was in the St John's Ambulance full time. As they were both out to work every day, and could be called out at any time, she was evacuated. Olive kindly contributed her own written account.

TEACHERS DID ALL IN THEIR POWER TO GET US TO STAY PUT

Olive

I was thirteen on the 27th April, 1940. On Sunday 2nd June, 1940 I was evacuated to Shirebrook in Derbyshire. I had chosen a friend, Jean, to pair up with but she returned to Lowestoft at Christmas 1940, so I was then on my own.

The day of the evacuation arrived. My case was packed a few days beforehand, together with my gas mask. I was excited about going at the time. I had never been away from Lowestoft. Many parents couldn't afford holidays. I had in mind that we wouldn't be away for long. It was said, 'It will all be over by Christmas,' and as a thirteen year old you believe those things.

I walked to Church Road Senior Girl's School with my mother. We said our goodbyes and Mother said, 'Now remember, be a good girl and remember to send a postcard to us when you are settled.' At that moment I did feel sad as she left, but all my friends were there and we soon got chatting away. We were lined up two by two, then we walked to the buses which took us to Lowestoft Railway Station. Parents were not allowed on the platforms. There were approximately 3500 on the platforms. I have often wondered how all this went so smoothly.

We settled in our carriages and away we left, I think about 10.50am. We arrived in Shirebrook at 4.45pm after a six hour journey feeling extremely hot and tired. We were then taken to Shirebrook Central School for tea and billeting. We walked and walked dropping girls off here and there. We came to Number 4 Brunner Avenue and were put in the charge of Mr and Mrs Moore, later to be called Auntie and Uncle. A truly lovely home. We certainly were with lovely people. We were so very tired.

Once in bed, I felt tearful, missing Mum and Dad. It was their custom to pop into my bedroom for a last 'goodnight'. I did sleep well after such a long, dramatic, and hot day. Next morning after breakfast, I wrote my postcard home, then went to the school room which had been allotted to us. My teacher was Miss Olive Read, a lovely lady. After the war and things were back to normal, I visited her at her house, and eventually in a nursing home until she passed away.

Of course at this time it was our summer holidays but every day teachers arranged various activities, rambles, swimming in Cresswell pool, and so on. Some evenings there would be country dancing, keep fit, or dramas in the church hall. Anything to keep us occupied. Although we had all these activities, I was very homesick. I missed Mum and Dad and the lovely North Sea breezes. Because it was still the summer holiday, we hadn't got our definite classrooms or teachers. We had a Miss Morgan, Mrs Rumbold, and Miss Read.

I was finally with Miss Read. Firstly I was with Miss Rumbold and at this time there were thirty two girls in the class. Just before we broke up for the Christmas break 1940, Miss Rumbold gave each girl a small picture with a few lovely lines. Mine read:-

'God bless thy year
Thy coming in,
Thy going out.
Thy rest, they travelling about,
The rough, the smooth, the bright the dear
God bless thy year.'

I thought what a wonderful thing to give us. I have always had this on show by the side of my bed ever since – Seventy nine years later I truly treasure it.

My foster father was a retired Deputy at the mine. He did take me down the shaft, just to get an idea what it was like. Even at such a young age, I felt very sorry for the men who had to work down there. Uncle Moore, as I called him, had a small finger bitten off by a pit pony. I felt so sorry for those ponies. When they were too old to work they were brought up to lovely fresh air, but often lost their sight. This upset me quite a lot.

As I looked out of my bedroom window I looked onto a massive slag heap; at regular intervals a huge bucket would tip up and release all the coal dust. This was happening day and night. Housewives, before hanging out their washing, would see which way the wind was blowing. If it was blowing in their direction, no linen could be hung out. If it was hung out it would come in black.

My foster mother loved the movies, my foster father didn't. One Saturday Auntie Moore asked if I would like to go with her to Mansfield (by bus) to the cinema there. Of course I jumped at the idea. So it was, that Auntie and I would on odd occasions see a good film. This was quite a highlight for me.

Auntie and Uncle had two sons and two daughters. One son was in the 8th Army. The other son lived in Shirebrook and was a miner. He would visit his mother every Saturday and quite often give me 6 pence which was at that time quite a lot for pocket money. Their eldest daughter was a midwife and the youngest daughter lived in Edwinstowe not too far from Shirebrook. I would be asked to go over there for a weekend and babysit on the Saturday night. They had a telephone and I was allowed to phone my mother back home. This was a lovely treat.

Auntie and Uncle Moore had a daughter-in-law in Epsom who had a son who was four years old. Epsom wasn't a safe place to be, so they evacuated to Shirebrook. I was in my element as I looked after the youngest when not at school.

Each Christmas I had a gift from Auntie and Uncle. First Christmas a silver serviette ring. When I married my husband, Jack, we were given a very pretty tray cloth which Auntie had embroidered, Auntie and Uncle treated me like one of their family. My mother and father each visited me twice (four visits) each stayed one week.

I did get home for Christmas 1940, 1941 and 1942. It was planned for me to come home one Easter but the bombing of Lowestoft was so bad I received a telegram to say 'stay put'. I was very disappointed but it was a sensible decision. Always when I did get home, there was a teacher to accompany me on the journey. One sad thing happened. One of my classmates came back to Lowestoft, I think the Christmas 1940, decided to stay and got a job in a shoe shop. During a raid the shop got a direct hit and she was killed. Such a shock. This was read out in assembly. Teachers did all in their power to get us to stay put.

Something wonderful we did achieve during our evacuation. We were told that our teachers were planning to put on an Operetta. This was called 'The Madcap Months'. Every teacher and every girl was involved. We all had a hand in making the clothes. The concert was such a great success. The audience, mainly foster parents and families, were really amazed at what we had achieved

My father stayed with me for a week. One of those days he took my friend, Violet, and me to Newstead Abbey, home to poet Lord Byron, and we had a wonderful time.

Another wonderful thing happened for me. Because I was away for three and a half years, I became the oldest girl in my class and should have found a place of work at that end. My headmistress knew I had thought of going in for shorthand and typing and she got in touch with the headmistress of the Shirebrook Central School and between them it was decided I would attend shorthand and typing. I cannot remember how long I was doing this but it was a good grounding for when I returned to Lowestoft. Once home I then attended and Anglo French School which also taught shorthand and typing. I was truly grateful for the help given me at the Shirebrook School. Yes, I did have loving foster parents, but oh it was so wonderful to be home.

I visited Shirebrook once for a holiday before I married. My husband, Jack. He and I also visited twice. Jack, was evacuated to Clowne, so we were able to visit his foster parents, also lovely people.

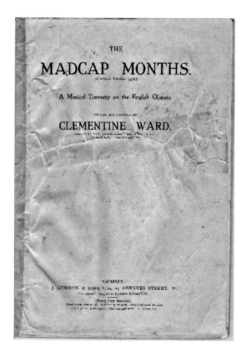

Olive's copy of the music to Madcap Months by Clementine Ward

Audrey Hales, (née Langley), was eight years old and attending Gorleston Road Primary School, Lowestoft when she was evacuated to Barlborough in Derbyshire with her older sister Brenda aged nine. Another older sister, Irene, went to Langwith and her two brothers went to Clowne.

YOU 'FUNNY' LOOK DIFFERENT!

Audrey front row second from the left

I was about eight and a half when I was evacuated. We were told that we were going away on a train and that was it, no explanation. I was with my sister, Brenda, who was a year older than me.

When we arrived in Barlborough and were in the hall it was a matter of 'pick, pick, pick, pick,' and we were among the last to be 'picked'. Brenda and I were together at first and had our own room with a big double bed.

We went to school at the Institute and when that closed we went to the local school. I was caned on more than one occasion. I remember one instance I was playing with one of the boys who lived near me at home in Fir Lane, Lowestoft. We were in the Institute kitchen and there was a lovely big fireplace. He said, 'Bet I can spit in that fireplace on the hot coals better than you'. So I did. The teacher came in and we were caught. She took me into the hall and slapped me. I was kept in after school that day too. I was also told off when I got home. They said, 'Where is the bread you were supposed to get on the way home from school?' Well, after being kept in, by the time I got to the shop, all the bread had gone. My foster mother went to school with me the next day to see the teacher. She said to the teacher, 'If you keep her in after school, or hit her again, I will pull every one the curls out of your head.' I was never kept in again and she never laid another hand on me. This foster mother stuck up for me but they left us on our own a lot. They used to go off all day and sometimes for weekends. They were in their early thirties and had one boy who was eight or nine months old. They would take him with them.

While they were away, we were left to play with the local children. Before they went, they would tell us that the back door was open and if we wanted something to eat, to go in and get it. We were sometimes playing out at night-time till about 10 o'clock. Eventually, they were 'spoken to' about that and we were moved. While we were at that billet we often had fleas and nits.

I was moved to Mr and Mrs Greeves and my sister Brenda went to Mr and Mrs Melbourne. The people in these two billets didn't have children of their own. We were then very happy because these second billets were good ones. My sister Brenda was next door and Mary Draper was the other side of her.

Sometimes, Mr Greeves used to bring me a 'pit biscuit'. It was as big as a saucer and took a long time to eat because it was hard. To begin with, I went back to play with the children near to the first billet and picked up nits again. Mrs Greeves lifted up my hair and cut it right off. That got rid of my nits! Mrs Greeves had a brother who worked on a farm and we sometimes went there. They were good people, Chapel people, and sang in the choir.

My mother came to see me once while I was there. She stayed with my sister Irene, who was twelve or thirteen years old, and in Langwith. Two of my brothers were in Clowne. Eventually the eldest two went back home because they were fourteen and due to leave school which meant they were no longer eligible to be evacuated. My eldest brother, who was not fit enough to be in the army, suddenly appeared, and took us home as well. That's the only train I can remember, the one coming home. It was full of air force and army personnel and we had to stand in the corridor or sit on suitcases all the way. We were away for about four years in all.

We then had to adjust to being home. After we had come home, a woman who knew me said to me, 'You funny look different'. Well, I got on my high horse. I had forgotten the local expression 'funny' meaning 'very', and said, 'What's wrong with me? I'm not funny.'

Once back in Lowestoft, I remember the doodlebugs came over while we were in a friend's house. I got up the next morning and I couldn't speak because it had frightened me so much. As I had lost my voice, my mother had the quietest fortnight she ever had!

When I left school, I went to work in the Gourock Ropework Company near the Hippodrome in Battery Green Road, Lowestoft. I earned nine shillings and nine pence a week as a braider.

I went back to Barlbourgh once when I was about eighteen. Mr Greeves was alive but Mrs Greeves had died. I have attended most reunions and together with Mary Draper (page 42) I organise the teas.

Foster parents Mr and Mrs Greeves on the left of the picture

Clive Capps was just five years old, one of the youngest evacuees, when he was evacuated from Dell Road Primary School in Oulton Broad, Lowestoft in June 1940 to Creswell in Derbyshire. His brother Carl, aged 7, travelled with him.

ROAD SIGNPOSTS TAKEN DOWN

Clive, Lowestoft Grammar School

When the government authorities classified Lowestoft as being at risk of bombing and invasion all schools were closed and, as a result, my parents Harry and Olive Capps eventually decided my brother Carl and I should be evacuated. For some reason my father, a coal merchant by trade and part time fireman in the war years, decided we should not go with the main party who went by train on 2nd June 1940. However, a few days later he took us by car to Creswell, the designated host village for pupils from three Lowestoft schools: Dell Road, Roman Hill and St. Andrews. This meant over 300 children arrived at Creswell village. We think the reason for our parents' change of mind was that, after first deciding we should not go, our house roof was badly damaged, so they feared the worst and changed their minds.

So we made the car journey which was nearly 200 miles. It must have been quite arduous for Carl and I as we had never travelled that far before. I remember very little about it but my brother told me at a later date that all the road signs had been taken down to confuse the Germans if they ever landed in England, which shows how serious the threat of invasion must have been – in fact we found out later that one of Hitler's plans was to land his army on the East Coast and then proceed to the City Hall in Norwich to make his victory speech on the impressive steps leading up to the main entrance.

When we arrived in Creswell we were sent to different billets and so I was separated from my brother Carl for the majority of the time away – he must have occasionally visited me as he is on one of the photos taken at Creswell.

First Billet

This was in Baker Street with a Mrs Biggins who was a rather large lady, very cheerful and friendly. She had a grown up daughter, Hilda. I was only there for a few weeks but it seemed much longer to me as a slightly nervous infant, first time away from home.

Perhaps the main memory of my stay there related to the fact that I did not like the crusts on bread – apparently I pulled them off and stuffed them in a drawer in the dining table and my secret was not discovered until weeks later, by which time they had gone rather mouldy – no reprimands as far as I remember. The other faint memory was playing in the lane outside with a girl called Margaret Holmes, who I did track down years later living in a nearby village, Whitwell.

Second Billet

Apparently after a few weeks I was moved on to a farmhouse which overlooked the world-famous archaeological site known as the Crags (previously spelt Craggs). This consisted of a number of ancient caves, tunnels and interesting rock formations.

At this house lived Mr and Mrs Boffey and their son John, aged 7. The timing of my arrival at the second billet can be very precise because, thanks to my mother, we discovered many years later a letter written to my mother by my foster mother Mrs Boffey on 9th July 1940 reassuring my mother that all was well.

John Boffey, Clive Capps and Carl Capps

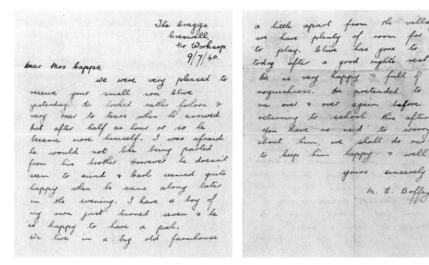

Letter dated 9th July 1940 from Mrs Boffey to Clive's mum

John, just two years older than me, was very friendly and made me feel very much at home – it would appear that as an only child he welcomed some company.

Next door (semi-detached) lived a little girl called Mary Blood, who was about 10, so I was lucky to have two young children close by. I had my own room as, being a farmhouse, it was quite spacious and there was a big courtyard where there was at least one dog. I do not remember much about my two-year stay at this well-situated billet in a very nice countryside setting.

Although we lived in a farmhouse I understand that Mr Boffey did work at the Creswell coal mine and his brother-in-law Amos Marple also had worked down the mine but had suffered a terrible accident and lost both legs. There is a photo of John and I with his dad and Amos where it is very apparent that Amos had lost his legs from the knee down – to me this became my most vivid first memory as a child. I was not scared and just accepted this fact that he had no legs.

The other memory was a reprimand from Mrs Boffey, who was a really nice lady, friendly but quite strict. For some reason, being naughty in some way I suppose, I was made to stand in front of a large grandfather clock in the hall and listen to the clock tick for a certain length of time – I survived and it did not, as far as I can remember, have any adverse effect on my stay.

My memories of my schooling are very scant. I vaguely remember the Creswell infant school situated at the bottom of the main road but due to a lack of space, as the village children took up most of the space, we were eventually moved to the Methodist Church in Mansfield Road, which in recent times was demolished. None of this was surprising when a village with a population of around 5000 had to deal with the influx of over 300 evacuee children overnight, which virtually doubled the school population. Eventually the local authorities developed a system whereby the local children went to school in the mornings and we, the evacuees, went in the afternoons. I am sure the local children thought that it was a plus feature of us arriving as they only had to attend school half time. Nevertheless my schooling must have suffered but it did not prevent me from returning home and eventually passing the exam for grammar school.

We were encouraged by the school and foster parents to write home from time to time and once again my mother had kept the letters I sent. At first these were very basic, not surprising me being aged only 5, but the writing gradually become more legible. Also, John Boffey wrote to my mother.

Overall I can say my stay was quite pleasant with good treatment from my foster familiy and living in very pleasant countryside surroundings.

Meanwhile, this unfortunately was not the experience my brother Carl went through. He was moved four times, through no fault of his own and bullied by the local boys, some of whom resented the arrival of these children with different accents from a place far away. I am pleased to say that I do not recall any 'bad' incidents for myself.

I do not remember associating with any other evacuees which was not surprising as I had only just started school at the Lowestoft end and at Creswell I was living at a farmhouse outside the main village. It seemed that I very much kept myself to myself and lived in my own world for that evacuee period.

My other memory related to the fact that most food stuffs were on ration, including sweets which would be of much interest at that age. I do remember going down to a shop in the main street and buying sweets and then going back home, changing my jumper, taking off my glasses and returning to the shop for a second lot of sweets and getting away with it!

Return Home

Eventually it was decided that I should return home mainly because of constantly catching colds which were blamed on the rather damp weather prevailing in Derbyshire at that time. So it therefore worked out I arrived back in Lowestoft in 1943 by which time we had moved house, as was always intended, from Wollaston Road, Central Lowestoft to Colville Road in Oulton Broad. I was unable to return to Dell Road School as it was occupied by troops, some from Belgium. Therefore I had to make a fairly long journey to Gorleston Road School which entailed a bus ride from the bottom of Colville Road.

I eventually went back to Dell Road School at the beginning of 1945 passed for Grammar School and took up my place the following year, by which time the war was over. However what I do remember about living in Colville Road was a huge bonfire on V.E. Day (8th May 1945) burning the wooden shutters which had been used to comply with the compulsory blackout of all lights in buildings during the war period.

In 1953 I obtained a place at Kings College London and three years later was awarded a BSc degree in chemistry. During my college holidays back home in Lowestoft, I met my wife-to-be Jean and we were married in 1957. We then moved down to Buckinghamshire where we went on to have three children, Susan, Richard and Robert. Eventually we returned to Norfolk in retirement and recently celebrated our diamond wedding anniversary.

Visits to the host villages in Derbyshire were made by the Lowestoft Evacuees Association of which I am a member by coach from year to year and in 2007 I went to Creswell with my brother Carl and on the same visit met with Mary Blood, the Creswell girl who lived next door to my second billet. I also met Enid Hibbert, another Creswell girl, whose mother took in evacuee Iris Day.

Through the years, I often wondered what had happened to John Boffey, the boy living in my second billet (farm house) and decided to try and find him. After asking around in Creswell and numerous phone calls, I tracked him down as living in Cardiff. So in October 2007, my wife and I met with John and his wife – a truly emotional and memorable reunion after 67 years.

Later that same year I became a member of the BEA (British Evacuees Association) situated close to Retford and at their AGM in 2009 met Michael Aspel, a patron of the BEA and former evacuee.

In 2008 with granddaughter Rose, a reception class teacher in Norwich, I visited my old school Dell Road in Oulton Broad on the occasion of their centenary celebrations and Rose and I also went up to London to visit the Imperial War Museum to view their WWII and evacuee exhibits. Then in September 2009 we attended a National Reunion of all evacuees held at St. Pauls Cathedral when over 1,000 evacuees attended to commemorate the start of the war 70 years earlier.

Noreen James, (née Boyce), was an only child. She was ten years old and attending Church Road Senior Girls School in Lowestoft when she was evacuated to Shirebrook, Derbyshire in June 1940.

SHE USED TO BE SUCH A LITTLE PUDDING

Noreen back row second from left, next to Miss Stevenson

My father had worked on the cruise shipping liners going to Australia and New Zealand and during the war he was in Burma. Therefore, for a lot of the time, it had been just Mum and me.

When I was evacuated, being an only child, I was alone. When we arrived in Shirebrook, we were (I have to use the word) 'herded' into a school, where we sat on the floor. I had the feeling that the people of the village didn't know beforehand that they would be receiving evacuees. Everything was done in such a hurry.

The people of the village walked back and forwards through the school hall and chose children as if they were choosing a dress in a shop. I'll have that one – no I don't want that one, I'll have that one. It made me feel as if we were not wanted. Looking back now, I feel it was not organised thoroughly enough. However, I'm not saying there was anything wrong with the village, or the people in it.

I was not taken in by anyone while I was sitting in the school hall. I had sat there for a long time, since the train arrived. Miss Stevenson was my teacher and she said to me, 'I haven't got a billet to go to either, so you and I will go for a walk and 'knock on doors'. So, she was knocking on doors asking people to take me in. Of course, they received money for taking in an evacuee and we eventually found me a billet. The couple who took me in didn't really want me. The woman said, 'All right, I'll take *it*.' Not 'I'll take the child.' I had to do my own washing, the ironing and get my own food. My grandmother had taught me to cook a little but I had no idea how to do the washing. I would keep my room clean, brushing the mats that were on the floor. The man of the house would take me into the garden and I had to dig for whatever food I wanted. Potatoes, carrots, any vegetables. He had an allotment and I would have to dig the allotment too. Although they were very hard, they never hit me, it was a different kind of hurt. My mother sent me three shillings per month. It doesn't sound like much now but at the time it was. It was to get toothpaste or anything else I needed. However I didn't ever receive it. My mother naturally thought I was being fed, but I wasn't. I didn't get the letters my mother sent with the money either. They opened them before I received them. Therefore, I didn't get any information at all.

One morning, the lady who lived opposite the house I was in, called across to me, 'Come over here dear', she said. 'How are you finding your billet? If you don't like it come over to me.' But I was only ten and I was too frightened. I said, 'I'm not allowed to. I have to stay where I've been put.' So she said, 'Now look! I want you to understand that this is not how we all are in this road.' Another lady, who was with her, said, 'If I could have the child, I would have her with me. She wouldn't be in there with them.' So, the neighbours were aware that I wasn't being looked after. I went to school but I never told Miss Stevenson how I was being treated. I just told my school friends.

Fortunately for me, one of my aunts had two children at nearby Wesley Vale. She came to visit them to make sure they were settled. She realised she wasn't far from Shirebrook, where I was, so she came on the bus to visit me. I was very pleased to see her. At the time, she didn't make me feel I was somewhere where I shouldn't be. She didn't make any remark about it to me. She never said she was going to tell my mum or that she would get me home. She simply went home. But once she was home, she said to my mother, 'If you don't get that child home now, you won't get her home at all. She's not being looked after. She has lost a lot of weight and looks as if she's ill. And she used to be such a little pudding.'

My Uncle Billy, my mother's youngest brother, was on leave from the Air Force. He said to my mother, 'I have a friend who has a car which I can hire and we'll go and bring Noreen home'. So, they came to get me. They decided not to announce they were coming, so I didn't know. When they arrived my uncle got out of the car and went to the house. He asked, 'Is Noreen here?' He was told that I was upstairs cleaning my bedroom. My mother didn't get out of the car at this point. He asked whether it was alright for him to go up and he did. They never even queried who he was. He could have been anyone. He said to me, 'Come on, you are coming home.' I didn't want to pack my bag. I didn't want to take anything. I just wanted to go home. My mother then got out of the car and collected my things.

When I got back, my mother took me to see the Doctor. The doctor was Doctor Richardson, he said that I was malnourished because I had not been fed properly. He told my mother not to fill me up with 'just anything', but to make sure to give me food that was nourishing.

Once I was home, my mother told me I would never need to leave again and would stay there with her. She was of the age when she should have worked in a war factory, but she wouldn't. She defied the 'powers that be', telling them that she wasn't going to leave her child. She said, 'Where I go, she goes.' The only way she could stay at home with me, and not work in a factory, was to provide a billet for sailors instead. She had quite a large house so she used to take in six and sometimes twelve sailors. They were wonderful. They helped Mum a lot. If there was an air-raid, they always made sure we were in the shelter before them. When I told my mother that they 'night time' bombed Sheffield and we could see the lights she said, 'Good grief, you might just as well have stayed at home as to go all that way to see bombs dropping.' I can remember seeing the 'Wallers Raid' taking place in Lowestoft.

There was nothing said by any of the authorities, when I came back home, as to why I had not stayed in Derbyshire or how I got home. Looking back, I don't think anything could have been done because, it would have been a child complaining about grownups and I wouldn't have been believed. I learnt from it. I can say it taught me right from wrong and when I had children, how to bring them up.

Miss Mallet, the teacher who was looking after my group of children, made a remark, reported in the Lowestoft Journal at the time, saying, that unfortunately not all the children had the opportunity of going into a house where they were wanted

My future husband, Harry, had been in the RAF and my Uncle Billy introduced me to him. Harry worked at the Eastern Coach Works in Lowestoft. I have a son, David, who works at CEFAS and a daughter, Denise, who is a radiographer at the Norfolk and Norwich Hospital.

Trudy James (née Boakes), was attending Church Road School, Lowestoft when she was evacuated, in June 1940, to Creswell, Derbyshire with her twin brother, Jack. Her older sister, Dorothy, was fifteen and went to Shirebrook just over six miles away. Her friend's name was also Dorothy.

DIVIDED LOYALTIES

Trudy on the right with foster parents Mr and Mrs Chadwick

I was eight when I went with my twin brother to Creswell, a very small mining village near Worksop. When we left by train, I waved out of the window to my auntie as we passed her house. I thought we were going for a holiday.

My friend, Dorothy, lived at the bottom of my road in Lowestoft and I kept close company with her. When we arrived in Cresswell we went to the big Odeon Cinema. We children were in twos and I was still with Dorothy. I was scared stiff because I was a bit timid. We were all in a line as we were walked down Welbeck Street. As we went along it was a case of one in there or two in there, all the way down. We stopped at a sweet shop and a woman said to me, 'You and Dorothy are in there.' I didn't really want to go in at the time. However, they were Mr and Mrs Chadwick and I had a really lovely billet with them. Dorothy cried so much that after a few weeks she went back home. I thought, 'Oh, she's gone home and left me all alone!'

Mr and Mrs Chadwick didn't have any children of their own and Mrs Chadwick wanted me to call her mum, which I did. She used to say she wanted to adopt me. I would say that I had a mum at home. But she wanted me to stay there. Sometimes I would get upset because they were so good and I didn't want to leave them. But I also wanted to see my mum. When my mum came to visit me I would hurry to her and call her Mum very quickly before Mrs Chadwick was close enough to hear.

My twin brother, Jack, was billeted in Dukes Head Street. I hardly ever saw him. My sister, Dorothy, was fifteen and went to Shirebrook with her school. I really wanted to see her so Mrs Chadwick took me to Shirebrook to look for her. We did find her, but I only saw her that once. My brother went home early because he wasn't happy.

I always went to church on Sunday. One Sunday, after Mrs Chadwick had bought me some new fur gloves, I lost one. I was there five years and that is the only time she told me off. When we went to church I wore a hat. I called it my 'Deanna Durbin' hat. I even wore it after I came home and everyone thought I had gone a bit 'funny'.

Mrs Chadwick had a sister who had a piano. I loved the fact that she allowed me to play it. I learnt to play 'You are My Sunshine'. The good news was that I never heard a siren throughout my stay.

Mr Chadwick used to say to Mrs Chadwick, 'You spoil her.' But she didn't take any notice of him. Perhaps he said that because he knew I would eventually go home and he was trying to prevent her from getting too close to me. I was very lucky as I know a lot of people didn't have very good billets. When we knew the time was coming for me to go home, Mrs Chadwick would say, 'You are not going are you?' Of course I did go home but I always kept in touch.

I married Ken James but the incredible thing was that his brother, Harry, also married an evacuee, Noreen James née Boyce. She became my sister in law and we have often attended evacuee reunions together.

I went back several times after the war with my husband and we took our children to see them. When Mrs Chadwick was ill, just before she died, I wanted to visit her. However, her family felt it would upset her too much. But, while I was living with her, she took me to the cemetery where all her family are buried. Although I have never visited I am happy that I know where her grave is.

From left to right Mrs Chadwick, Trudy, Trudy's friend Joyce and Mrs Chadwick's sister

Peter Chenery was nine years old when he was evacuated with Roman Hill Juniors School, Lowestoft on 2nd June 1940, to Creswell in Derbyshire. He had one brother, Jack, who was five years older. Jack was too old to be evacuated and was employed at Robertson's Boatyard.

I COULD SEE THE GERMAN PILOT IN THE COCKPIT

Peter

When we arrived at the cinema in Creswell, I was one of the last to be picked out. A comparatively young couple took me. The man of the house was a miner. I didn't see much of him at all as he was working long hours. They had a boy two years younger than me. I shared a bedroom with him but I had my own bed.

I went to the local school which we shared with the local children. Due to there being so many extra children, each school went for a half day only. My teacher from Lowestoft, Miss Crawford, didn't come with us

109

but we had Lowestoft teachers who did make the journey. While I was there we got frequent visits from a young girl who was about eleven, and lived next door. I think I may have been getting special attention from her because I was an evacuee. I think she was intrigued by my accent and was interested in me simply because I wasn't a Creswell boy.

We used to play in the Creswell Crags. Looking back it was a very dangerous thing to do and we were completely unsupervised. The rocks were covered with moss and therefore very slippery. If you slipped off one it could have been horrendous. They are fenced in now and you have to pay to get in. While I was there I spent time with the Boggis twins from Lowestoft.

At the time of the outbreak of war, my father was the Landlord of the Triangle Tavern, in St Peter's Street, Lowestoft, but he also worked as a delivery driver for E Pordage a wholesale grocers and fruitier. A lot of his time was taken up with ripening bananas. They were the agents for Fyffe bananas and the bananas used to arrive in bunches straight off the tree. They had two specially made rooms at their store in Tennyson Road, Lowestoft that were insulated and heated. My father used to take the bunches, hang them on hooks, and after a day or two they would start to turn yellow. They were then packed in boxes two or three foot long and he would drive them to the shops.

After I had been evacuated for four months, E Pordage closed down their branch in Lowestoft and moved my father to Cambridge. Cambridge was regarded as a safe area, so I was brought back home again. Not that I minded. Although the people, who looked after me were kind their son, who was two years younger than me, was constantly trying to get me into trouble. I was being accused, of doing things that I didn't do. He was a really nice looking little boy, with blond wavy hair, like bubbles in the Pears Soap advert.

When it came time for me to leave Creswell, the lady came to see me off. What really, really, surprised me was the fact that she burst into tears when it was time to say goodbye. I thought, well, she obviously must have thought something of me. However, she didn't give that impression while I was living with her. I didn't come straight back to

Lowestoft, I went to Cambridge, where my father was working. I travelled on my own from Creswell to Cambridge, at age ten.

After a while, I don't know whether he was forced to change his job because the E Pordage branch closed, or he was directed to work for a firm that was a subsidiary of Lever Brothers. Most of the Lever Brothers products were rationable goods, so it was a sort of bonded warehouse and he was the warehouse foreman. They were rationed goods, so the goods had to be looked after. Pilfering had to be prevented and there were strict controls.

At Milton, just outside Cambridge, father used to do fire watch overnight. So they had camp beds in the office and I would sleep there with him. If any incendiary bombs dropped on the warehouse, it was the job of the fire watches to put the fires out.

When we were at Cambridge, we were listening to Lord Haw-Haw[1], on the radio one night, and he said; because the allies had bombed one of the University towns in Germany, there would be a retaliatory raid on one of our university towns. We didn't know which one it would be, but it turned out to be Cambridge. All the bombs were dropped down the main shopping street. As it happened during the night and all the shops were closed, there were very few casualties. When London was being bombed, from where we lived, you could see the glow in the sky in the direction of London sixty miles away.

Our street backed onto a street called Coldhams Lane. Beyond Coldhams Lane, was the outskirts of Marshalls Aerodrome. During the war it was used as a training base for RAF pilots. They learned to fly in De Havilland Tiger Moth biplanes there. One afternoon, when I was in my back garden, I saw a plane come over and it started machine-gunning the tiger moths, on the aerodrome. It came in low and I could see the German pilot in the cockpit.

They reopened E Pordage and my father went back as Manager. I was supposed to go to the grammar school as I had scraped through the

---

[1] William Joyce, aka Lord Haw Haw was a notorious broadcaster of Nazi propaganda to the United Kingdom during World War 11.

Scholarship. I went to the Central School in Cambridge. If you did well, you we were sent to the County Grammar School. If you did even better than that, you went to Perse College for Boys.

The war was still on in Japan when I came back to Lowestoft. I was friends with the Boggis twins, Basil and Gordon, who had been in Creswell and whose father had a butcher shop, on the corner of Raglan Street. I started going out with the 'Boggis twins' and also a chap named Dick Spelling. I joined the Boston Lodge Youth Club and Jean the 'Boggis twins' sister taught me to dance. I spent lots of time at the Palais de Dance, at Pakefield. I married Eileen Pickering and we went on to have two children.

I didn't go to the grammar school. I got myself a job, at the Eastern Coach Works where I stayed for six months. I wanted a job where I worked with wood and the buses had wooden frames. I moved on to the Harbour Works and was called up for the RAF. I went to Fasburge in Germany. Eventually, I became a lecturer in carpentry and joinery at Lowestoft College and became a colleague of another Lowestoft evacuee, Melville Canham.

Recently, I have been back to Creswell with the Lowestoft Evacuee Association trips. On the first trip, I made back to Creswell, with Chris Brookes and others from the Lowestoft Evacuee Association; we went to the Crags. We were going to go in, but because the price was so high, we didn't. I couldn't remember where I actually stayed in Creswell when I went back on that trip. The second time I went, Chris was kind enough to take me on a round trip of Creswell and I think I found the house I stayed in then. I now belong to a music appreciation group with another evacuee, Kathleen Wilton. I am a Baritone and belong to four choirs.

Pauline 'Peggy' Knight, (née Cook), was fourteen and attending Church Road School in Lowestoft when she was evacuated to Langwith in Derbyshire. She went with her brother, Peter, who was eight, and her sister, Pamela who was five. She also travelled to Langwith with her friend Agnus 'Sissy' Butcher.

IT SEEMED THE BEST DRESSED CHILDREN WERE PICKED FIRST

Peggy at the back with Peter and Pamela

I can't remember crying or anything. I just took it in my stride. In fact, I went to school very excited. As children, we didn't see the seriousness of the war. I remember one Sunday morning the siren sounded when my friend, Sissy, and I were climbing on Church Road School railings. We were frightened so we ran to a nearby lady's house and asked if we could get under her table.

My mum had a dream that the Germans were invading Lowestoft so she signed us up to be evacuated. I was with my friend, Sissy, on the train to Langwith. We wanted to stay together but that didn't happen. She went to another billet and I didn't see her again.

When we arrived, we were taken to Langwith Junction Central School and given refreshments. People came in and picked out which children they wanted. It was awful. It seemed that the best dressed children were picked first. I had promised my Mum that I would keep my young sister, Pamela, who was only five, with me. So, I had to make sure that happened.

Pamela and I were billeted with Mrs Barker who was in the WVS and we went to Whaley Thorn School where we got on well with the local children. The day we arrived, Mrs Barker had us sleep in a cupboard because they thought they were going to be bombed. I remember hoping they wouldn't shut the door! After that we had a proper bed. It was a very good home but she was very strict and wouldn't allow me to do things like go dancing with my friends. They were older people and their own children were grown up. Even though there was a war on we were well fed. I remember the elderberry tree in the garden and how she used to make elderberry fruit puddings.

When we were first there, my brother, Peter, had a terrible billet. He was nine. It was said that the woman he was billeted with, would sing in public houses and eat tripe on the bus! Whatever happened, he was badly treated, and he won't talk about that billet. Mum came to see us after four weeks. She hired a taxi, sharing the fare with another mother. When mother saw where Peter was, she found him another billet.

I was playing 'Queenie Queenie Catch the Ball' in the road on the second day I was in Langwith. I saw a curtain move in the house opposite. I little then knew, that the boy who was looking out of the window would one day be my husband, Hardy. He was ill with rheumatic fever at the time, so didn't come out to speak to me. He was three years older than me and we eventually spent a lot of time together. However, Mrs Barker was very strict. I was babysitting one day and he wanted to meet me. He gave my brother a note to give to me. Peter lost the note and someone picked it up and gave it to Mrs Barker. That got me into trouble because it said, 'I'll come and meet you tonight and I'll give you something I have always wanted to give you.' That was a kiss! When I got in Mrs Barker told me to sit down. I thought 'There's something wrong here.' She told me off and I cried.

After that, I told Hardy that if it was going to cause that much fuss, we had better not speak to each other anymore.

When I started work, Mrs Barker said she couldn't keep us because she couldn't look after my little sister while I was at work. She was busy in the WVS. So, I found Pamela somewhere and I went to where my brother was billeted. They were the Walkers and were related to Hardy although I didn't know that at the time.

Hardy and I met up again later after he had gone into the army. I was out one day and looking after a little girl who I had in a pushchair. Hardy's dad came along and told me that Hardy was home. He had been shot by friendly American fire. The wound was an inch away from an artery. He was in Wolverhampton Hospital and I went to see him there. After that we started to see each other again. At the time, if soldiers had been wounded, they wore a blue suit and red tie so that people knew. This meant we sometimes got preferential treatment as appreciation, for example, at football matches.

When I first left school I was living in Langwith. I got a job in Mansfield working at Woolworths. Hardy suggested we go to Lowestoft for a week. Woolworths wouldn't let me have the time off, so I asked for my 'cards'. After that trip to Lowestoft, I went back to Langwith and went to work at British Home Stores and I was supervisor there. Going to work in the mornings, I had to cross a field to get to the bus stop to Mansfield. There was a bull chained up in that field. I used to have to pass that bull every morning. I certainly remember that!

Eventually, I got restless and wanted to go home to Lowestoft. There was a job going in True Form Shoe Shop and my mum went in and asked them to keep it open for me. My friend had already got a job there and my mum knew I would like to work with her. This was Sissy who I was on the train with when we were first evacuated. My dad was a bit more cautious than my mother who didn't see danger in anything. The war was still on and Dad said 'On no account is she coming home'. What a blessing for me. However, Sissy was already back in Lowestoft and working in the shoe shop. She was in the 'Wallers Raid' of 13th January 1942. As we were such good friends, I would have been there with her, sure as eggs are eggs. She was buried for sixteen hours and died in hospital that night. I was still in Langwith. I received a letter she had posted to me on the morning of the raid. I can remember what she said in it. 'I just knitted myself a green fluffy hood. You will have to make yourself one, Peggy.'

I came home in 1944, when I was eighteen, to join up for war work. My mother was having another baby, my brother, Paul. At that time, there were Doodle Bugs to worry about. I had been away for five years.

It worked out well for me. The boy from Langwith and I were married in Lowestoft and had three lovely children. He was a wonderful husband. Being evacuated changed my life completely.

We went back every year with our children and would go and visit Mrs Barker as well as my mother-in-law. The second time we went back, we walked up to where I used to live with the Walkers and I have a photo of me pointing to what was my bedroom window.

My brother, Peter, returned to Langwith with one of the reunion trips after the war. He met up with the lad he stayed with in his second billet. That lad died soon after. They used to play me up something awful, hanging tin cans over my bed. My sister, Pamela, also came back to Lowestoft to live.

Pauline centre back with her foster parents, Peter and Pamela

Ethel Mclellan (née Field), was one of three sisters evacuated from Lowestoft to Whitwell in Derbyshire in June 1940. Daisy was the oldest, Ethel was in the middle age ten, her younger sister Grace, was eight. Their foster parents had a daughter, Theo aged nine.

MOTHER'S HOUSE WAS BOMBED

From left to right Daisy, Grace, and Ethel

When I and my two sisters, Daisy and Grace, were evacuated, we looked on it as an adventure. We had never been anywhere before, people didn't in those days. My older sister, Daisy, went to Notley Road School and we all got on the bus there to take us to the railway station. There were so many children going that day! Parents weren't allowed to come to the station to see us off, although some did apparently.

My Mum wasn't going to send us in the first place, but after a bomb fell on Lowestoft she changed her mind. My younger sister and I were lucky to be able to keep with our older sister. We two were at Lovewell Road School, and the children there went to Glossop. When they found out that they shouldn't split families up, to keep us together with Daisy we went with the group to Whitwell instead of going to Glossop.

When we were billeted, because there was three of us, we were the last ones chosen. I haven't come across another case where three were taken in together. The lady that took us in, Mrs Kirk, didn't want three but she took us all on a temporary basis. I didn't know it at the time but at first, the family said if any of us was to move somewhere else it would be the middle one, which was me. This was because if they just kept two, the oldest could then look after the youngest. But we all stayed there the whole time.

We were very lucky we had a lovely billet. We thought Mrs Kirk was strict but she was lovely with it. Our billet was in Southall Cottages which was like a courtyard. There were five houses and we were in the third one. We had to cross the courtyard to go to the outside toilet, but it was a flush toilet. They had a washroom at the end of the row of houses with a copper. We also used this washroom to have our baths.

Mr and Mrs Kirk had one daughter, Theo. Theo was aged nine, in-between my young sister and me. I was ten and my young sister, Grace, was eight. So, we were all a similar age and all got on well. We had our ups and downs like most people do but we got through and we stayed there all of the war. We didn't have any toys to take with us but Theo had lots of toys so we played with hers. I used to play with a little black doll and I loved her. When I had children of my own I realised that to take on three other children; that was a lot.

Our father was a sawyer and worked at Jewson's. This was different to Mr Kirk who was a butcher. During the war Mr Kirk also worked down the pit a few days a week. In the house there was a cellar, and when the air-raid siren went we went down there. We also played down there sometimes. You would laugh at this now, but at the time we used to have an electric fire with an electric bar and we used to put water in a little can and heat it on the electric fire. They told us not to do that!

While we were there we went to our first wedding and also our first pantomime at Sheffield. We saw Cinderella. We had never seen anything like it in our lives. Jack Buchannan was Buttons, he was the star, but I can't remember who the others were. Mr Kirk's sister got married while we were there. I have a photograph of us, and I think it was taken before we went, because we are all done up smart. We were very poor and we thought Mr and Mrs Kirk were rich.

Mrs Kirk had a front room and she used to roll the carpet out and teach us to dance. We went to the Manor House to dances on a Saturday night and learnt the military two-step, veleta, and the waltz. We had to do an hour's knitting every night, we all had a part of a jumper to knit. I hated it because I was forced to do it, but it got the thing done. We also went to church once on Sundays.

She did look after us well, Mrs Kirk. We were better off there than when we were at home because mother had another two children who were younger than us. They were not old enough to be evacuated.

To start with, when we went to school we only went to the village school for half a day. The other half of the day we went outside into the woods or playing fields. We had lessons outside sometimes if it was fine enough. Later we went to school in the Miners' Welfare Hall. We had three different classes for the different ages. There was a little room upstairs and we would go up there and listen to current affairs on the wireless with the teacher.

I always remember Rita Smith. She went to Glossop to start with, then came to Whitwell. We used to play two balls up against somebody's wall. Rita and I sometimes meet at reunions.

It's a good thing we did go away, because my mother's house was bombed. Nobody was in it thankfully. If we hadn't been evacuated someone would have been in that house at the time. Because of the house being bombed mother had to move. After she moved she had another baby, Muriel. We didn't see that baby until she was four years old, because mum couldn't afford to come to see us, and anyway travel was restricted in war time.

My mother came up to see us after the war, before we came home, but never during the war. It was a long time for me not to see my mother. I think if anything like that had happened when my children were small I would have gone with them. Not that we weren't happy, we were, but the heartstrings pulled.

At the end of the war we came back to Lowestoft, because you all had to come back. But we liked it up there so we returned again later. Eventually my older sister, Daisy, married and lived there permanently.

I still have a niece there now. We keep in touch with Mrs Kirk's granddaughter, and just over a year ago, when my husband died, my niece and Mrs Kirk's granddaughter came to Lowestoft for the funeral. I was very pleased they came.

We wrote home every week and were each given a page of paper. We always used to say 'bags' the pad, because it was easier to write on the pad. We probably only wrote a paragraph each. I kept up the writing for forty years. My eldest sister, who went back to live there, used to write every week. When my mother could no longer write I used to go to see her every Sunday, read Daisy's letter to her, and write back. After my mother died, despite the fact that we had a phone, I continued to write to my oldest sister until she died in 2013. I really miss doing that.

When we first went back to Whitwell after the war, my older sister, Daisy, and my younger sister, Grace, worked for Mr Kirk, delivering meat. I went back again to live with somebody who wanted 'live in help', a 'dog's body' really. They had a milk round and I used to take the milk out at 5.30am. It meant me tipping the milk from the great big churns into the gallon, and taking it to the door to dish out in pints. Blooming cold! I couldn't wear gloves for that job even in the winter and my hands froze. I earned my keep plus was paid pocket money. I stayed about five years. I was nearly twenty-one when I eventually came back to Lowestoft and met my husband, Gordon, who was in Royal Navy at the time.

When the Lowestoft Evacuee Association ran outings back to Derbyshire, my husband and I went nearly every time. I noticed that lovely Derbyshire stone the houses are built of. As children we didn't notice how nice they were. It has got too much for me now, to go back. When you get old you find you can't do the things you want to do. It was always lovely to visit. They made us so welcome even after the war. Being evacuated made a big difference to how my life turned out.

From left to right Theo (foster mother's daughter),
Daisy, Ethel and Grace

John Clarke was seven years old, living in Notley Road, Lowestoft, and attending Lovewell Road School, when he was evacuated to Glossop in Derbyshire in June 1940. He had three sisters Sheila, Eileen, and Maureen the youngest.

CHOCOLATE FROM SAULT ST MARIE

John back right with three sisters Sheila, Eileen and Maureen

I was seven when I was evacuated with my sister Sheila, who was eighteen months younger than me. On the way, on the train, we were each given some chocolate. I found out later it came from a chocolate factory in Sault St Marie, a town in Ontario, Canada. I think Sault St Marie adopted Lowestoft and arranged for the chocolate to be delivered.

Two Teachers, Mrs Gosling and Mr Price, came with us. We used to call Mrs Gosling 'Goose Gog'. The teacher in my class was Mrs West. I can remember the air-raid shelters were under the big square playground at Lovewell Road School.

I believe us children had already been allotted to foster parents. I don't remember being picked. I was billeted with Edith and Tom Hurst. Mr

Hurst worked in Fieldings the jewellers and his wife, Edith, was an usherette at the Empire Cinema in Glossop across the road from Fieldings. My foster parents had a daughter, Margaret, who eventually came to Lowestoft to live (see story below).

The billet was a terraced house. It's strange the things you remember. The streets were set out in a diamond shape. I had my first bicycle and I can remember riding down towards the point of the diamond and on that point there was a big double gate to a builder's yard. As I came up nearly to it, something went 'beep beep beep'. I thought it was a car and fell off my bike. But, another little boy came round the corner on a bike, calling out, 'beep beep beep'.

There was a road, off Hollingcross Lane, and it had a curve and a stream running down near a big rope mill. I remember, one day, coming home and going down to Slate Lands, now Slate Lands Road. Near the river, there were ducks. I was on my own and I saw all these ducks and the nest on the ground. So, I took the ducks eggs home. We probably ate them, because food was rationed.

I went to Littlemore School, at the bottom of Victoria Street in Glossop. I was a loner so didn't mix well and can't remember the local boys. I can still see the school now though, the playground and the shape of it. I remember Manor Park. To get into Manor Park there was a gate with two steps. I can remember those two steps even now. Apparently, Manor Park is still there.

At the bottom of Victoria Street, where the train station was, there was a big layby where the buses to Manchester would stop. They were blue and on them they had HMLSD, Hayde Mottom Stalybridge Joint Services. I can't believe I remember that!

My mother, Alice, visited and stayed on one occasion. I didn't come back to Lowestoft until I was eleven and had been away about five years. Coming home was just being moved yet again. It was just another train. When I came back, at first, I went to Notley Road School. I took the scholarship examination and passed to go to the Grammar School. There was a further screening, before you got in, and we were interviewed. I didn't pass that interview. I believe they wouldn't accept me because my father was a fisherman.

My father, Edward, known as Teddy, was a Chief Engineer in the Royal Navy on the 'Right Admiral' and was at the Normandy Landings in June 1944. He said that if any ships were blown up and the sailors fell into the sea, the other British ships couldn't stop to pick them up because they would have been shot at. So, British sailors were in the water waving to them but they had to go right past. He was based in Reykjavik, in Iceland, after the war.

After being in the Merchant Navy, I became a steward on P & O Cruises and married my wife, Maureen. We had a daughter, Sarah and a son, Steven, who we lost in a road accident at Potter Heigham in Norfolk.

I went back to Glossop once, after the war for a holiday, and found it had changed a great deal.

John top left, back in Lowestoft with his three sisters
and mum and dad

MARGARET

Margaret comes from Glossop. John Clarke (above), was billeted with her parents, when he was evacuated there from Lowestoft on 2nd June 1940.

REVERSED ROLES

Margaret with her mother

My mother worked as an usherette in The Empire Cinema, in Glossop. She left there and went to the cotton mills. Eventually, she contracted T.B (tuberculosis). Children couldn't stay with people who had T.B. and therefore I had to move away and they needed to find me somewhere to live. As John Clarke had been billeted with my parents while he was evacuated our parents knew each other. So, I then went to live with his parents in Lowestoft. John was in the Merchant Navy by then and that is why they had room for me.

I thought Lowestoft was a beautiful place. I loved the beach and sea. I also loved the family environment, because as I was an only child that is something I didn't have at home. It was a comfortable home and John's parents were so kind to me. I had my seventh birthday in Lowestoft and I went to Lovewell Road School. I remember the little sweet shop across the road from the school. I stayed with John's parents for a year. I went back home when I was about eight, then my mother contracted T.B. again, and I went to live with an aunt.

We remained friends with John's parents after the war. Each year, they would visit us in Derbyshire and we would also visit them in Lowestoft.

When I was seventeen, I came to Lowestoft to lodge with Alice, John's mother, again. I met my husband, Fred, while I was living in Lowestoft this time and got married from John's mother's house. I was going to go home, to Glossop, to get married and arranged for my banns to be read there. I booked six weeks leave from work but my plans changed and I got married at Gunton St Peter's Church in Lowestoft.

I would go back to visit my parents and always thought I would go back to Glossop to live. But I decided Lowestoft was my home. I would like to take my grandchildren back to Glossop, to see where I was born.

Alma Mingay, (née Long), was six years old and the youngest of three siblings who were evacuated from Lowestoft to Glossop in June 1940. Her sister, Miriam, was two years older than her and her brother, Joe, was five years older. They had a baby sister, Marina who stayed in Lowestoft with their mother.

KEEP YOUR BALANCE AND PEDAL

Alma

My sister, Miriam, and I went to Lovewell Road Girls School and my brother, Joe, went to Lovewell Road Boys School. We were split up when we got to Glossop. My brother, Joe, went with Mr and Mrs Palmer and my sister went with another family in Glossop High Street who had a big sweet shop.

At my first billet the foster parents had a boy and a girl of their own. I wasn't there very long because I wet the bed and was therefore moved on.

I then went to Mr and Mrs Bordon. They had two boys who were older and had started work. I was spoilt and pampered by them.

We went to school and met up with local children and we mixed well. I couldn't ride a bike and I remember being at the top of a hill, when the other children from the village put me on a bike and said, 'Keep your balance and pedal'. At the bottom there was a horse trough and I went straight into the horse trough. As the house was at the top of the hill we had a sleigh when it snowed. We had a lot of fun and I loved the clogs they wore in that part of the country. I was with a good family. Mrs Bordon would say, 'I'm your second mum,' and I used to call her Mum.

My brother, Joe, being older than me, started his working life in a textile mill in Derbyshire. He then met his wife, stayed there, and they had two sons.

My father was a Lowestoft man and a fisherman. He went to Fleetwood, in Lancashire and Mother got accommodation there. He was torpedoed off Fleetwood and badly burnt. I can remember him going into Fleetwood hospital.

We came back from Fleetwood to live in St John's Road, Lowestoft. While we were there Mother took in forces personnel. From there, we moved to 22 Cleveland Road[1] which was near my Aunt Nellie. Cleveland Road has always been home to me. We were married in St. John's Church, which was our preferred choice. After we got married we left Cleveland Road and moved into a flat in London Road but I missed Cleveland Road as my grandparents had lived there.

In May 1947 my father, when he was only 47 years old, was lost at sea with all the crew on board the S.D.J., off Lowestoft. We never found out the truth about what happened, whether it was blown up or run down. There wasn't a single crew member's body found. The only thing they picked up was the lifebelt from the wheel. I have the death certificate, it says missing presumed drowned at sea. So we have no grave. The memorial service was held in The Bethel in Lowestoft.

My son, Steven was awarded the MBE for bravery in 2006. In 2005 he was working as a senior Police Officer in London on the day of the 7th July terrorist attacks where over 50 people were killed. He was

[1] This is the road in Lowestoft where Michael Caine had a bedsit very early in his acting career so that he could go on stage at the Arcadia Theatre in Lowestoft.

the first police officer to reach the bombed tube train on the Piccadilly line. He went down the escalator and entered the section of the tube train where the bomb had exploded and did his best to rescue and calm the passengers. As a result he went to Buckingham Palace the next year to receive his award directly from the Queen and he took me with him to the Palace – a proud day as a mother.

I went back to Glossop many times with the trips organised by the Lowestoft Evacuee Association. Finally in June 2017 a group of us went back on a memorable trip to Glossop. The Friends of Glossop Railway (Neil Williams) had arranged for a plaque to be made and displayed permanently on Glossop station to commemorate the arrival of the 600 Lowestoft evacuees in 1940. Bryan Howard and I had the honour of unveiling the plaque and there is a similar plaque displayed on Lowestoft Railway Station.

Alma's foster parents Mr and Mrs Bordon

Gladys Reynolds, (née Smith), was evacuated from Lowestoft in June 1940 to Whitwell in Derbyshire. She was thirteen. Her sister Rita, who was ten, went to Glossop and eventually to Whitwell.

A DOUBLE SEATED TOILET!

Gladys in Whitwell 1942

I was thirteen and attending Notley Road School when I was evacuated. Dad came to the station to see us off. Mum didn't come because she was too upset. I can remember Dad saying goodbye and waving. I watched him for as far as I could through the train window.

We children were told to pair off. There was some discussion about who wanted to be with who. I was with my friend Joyce, who was a good runner. She always won all the races.

When we got to Whitwell, the billeting officer had a list of people who were going to take in evacuees. Mrs Horne wanted two girls, so Joyce and I went with her. We called her 'Nanny' and called Mr Horne 'Grandad'.

I remember a very hot summer and a cold, hard winter. When the snow was on the ground all you could see, coming down the High Street, was the grey green buses for Sheffield. The boys had sledges and would ride down so fast that they went on up the hill on the other side.

Joyce and I shared a bed. There was another room, but newspapers were laid down on the floor and apples where kept in there. They had what they called an orchard. It was only two trees really, one sweet apple and one Bramley cooking apple. I think Grandad used to count the apples on the tree.

Nanny said one day, 'You mustn't touch them because Grandad knows exactly how many are on the tree'. So, the apples got the spare room and we children had to share. The next door neighbours had a beautiful Victoria apple tree. One year it was like a weeping willow it was so laden with fruit.

Before you got to Nanny and Grandad's orchard, there was a double outside toilet that was shared with a neighbour. It didn't have two separate seats, it was just a plank of wood with two holes in it. When we went there Joyce and I used to sit side by side chatting. Nanny and Mrs Hardwick next door took it in turns to keep it clean. It was scrubbed clean as a whistle. My mum said, 'At least you are in a clean billet'. Men used to come up the drive with a horse and cart and would shovel the contents into the cart.

Nanny and Grandad kept pigs but by the time we arrived they had killed the last one and the pigsty was empty. In the kitchen there was a walk-in cupboard with a huge marble top table. There was also three huge iron hooks to hang the pigs on after they had been slaughtered. I still remember those hooks in that big larder.

In the scullery next to the kitchen there was a pump and we used to wash our hair there. It was rain water and Nanny had a stocking she would put on the end of the pump to filter the water.

We went to Whitwell School and some children were not getting on with the local children. Miss Munnings, the Headmistress, who came with us from Lowestoft, had a word with the Council and they decided the children had better be separated. So from then on, we went to Hodthorpe, a very small village nearby. We were taught in a church at first and later moved on to a Chapel in Welbeck Street. I was in the choir and we went to several different places to sing.

Miss Edgerly was my class teacher to start with but her mother, who lived in Lowestoft near the Morning Star public house, became ill and she went home to look after her. Then I had Miss Risen. Miss Risen took us to Creswell for swimming lessons. I wouldn't dive off the board but she encouraged me which meant I got my proficiency certificate.

Eventually, my sister Rita was with us too. Mum hadn't wanted us to be parted from each other, but Rita went to Glossop which was a long way from Whitwell. Lots of children had been told by their mums to keep together but it didn't always happen. We had two cousins who went to Clowne: Ronnie Calver and Noel Brown.

Joyce and I only had the one billet. Mum came up to be with us for a time. She couldn't stay with us at Nanny and Grandad's because Miss Munnings said mothers were not allowed to be with the foster parents. Mum and Nanny got on well and Nanny wouldn't have minded. But someone said something and next thing we knew Miss Munnings came to the house and said Mum had to find other accommodation. This she did. She stayed with Mrs Allen in Portman Street and then moved to near the old mill in Mill Road, before going home again.

Suddenly Joyce said her Dad was coming for her. It was a surprise. Also my sister Rita left and went to Worksop. After they had left, I felt a bit lonely on my own. Mum or Dad wrote a letter to Nanny and said they thought I should come home and they came and fetched me. I was relieved really. Nanny and Grandad were good and I loved them both. I didn't dislike being away, I enjoyed the lovely hills, but I did miss my mum. I was fifteen in the March and returned home in July 1942.

After I came back to Lowestoft, Mum and I were walking along London Road South, when suddenly there was machine gun fire. Mr Peck at the shoe shop near the corner of Carlton Road, opened his front door and called us in. We had been told that if ever we were machine-gunned we should drop down and lie in the gutter. There were two young sailors behind us and they had done that, dropped down in the gutter. We could see the plane and we could see the gunner. There were lots of windows broken. It was awful. Mother was worried that Dad would be concerned about us so, as soon as things quietened down, we thanked Mr Peck and left. Dad was at the clinic carrying out his First Aid Duty. He had been in the First World War and was too old for the Second.

I got on well at school when I was away and got a good report. This provided a good reference when I wanted a job. I started at a little electrical shop in Lowestoft. There wasn't much to do. They would say, 'bring your knitting'. After that I went to Woolworth in South Lowestoft, opposite the Grand Cinema. I married Richard who was a shipwright.

I think being evacuated made me more independent. If you are at home you depend on your parents a lot more.

From left to right, Mr Horn, Joyce, Gladys and Mrs Horn

Bryan Howard was seven years old and living in St John's Road, Lowestoft, not far from the beach, when he was evacuated to Glossop in June 1940. He then went on to Worksop. Not having any siblings he made the journey alone.

SIX BILLETS IN ALL!

Bryan Howard

I was attending Lovewell Road School in Lowestoft. Everyone else at the school seemed to be going away and being evacuated. So, I wanted to go too. My parents weren't over keen but they could see the sense of it.

After eighty years, I can recall very little of the journey to Glossop. However, we must have travelled via Sheffield, as I remember being suddenly plunged into darkness then emerging from the Woodhead Tunnel into sunny countryside. The countryside was divided by stone walls, not hedges as we were used to. It's closed now, but the tunnel is between Sheffield and Manchester. It must have been a dreadful thing to build because there is a graveyard nearby where the people who were killed building it are buried.

As I was an only child I was on my own. I was one month short of eight and I remember, when we arrived at Glossop, it was a lovely sunny evening. In retrospect, I realise that the reception and billeting were very well organised. We were all soon allocated to our new foster parents. We arrived in the early evening and everyone was sorted by dusk.

As I was on my own, it was easy to find me a billet. Four of us children were sent in a car up to a hall, where the library is in Glossop, and we were dispersed from there. It was my first trip in a car. We had been earmarked to go to Manor Park Road.

I don't remember the name of the people I was billeted with but they lived right opposite Manor Park. They were middle class people. I think it was a social complication that had not really been grasped, that a lot of the evacuees from Lowestoft were very poor, and where they ended up was a matter of chance. My cousin, Dorothy, who is a little older than me, went to North Road with people who taught her good manners etc. Her name in those days was Dorothy Howard, she is now Dorothy Dew.

The people I was first billeted with, had a son and a daughter but I was the only evacuee. I wasn't there long, before I was moved to another billet, in Old Glossop. Again, I can't remember the name of the people I stayed with. But I remember the snow. Of course, because you are small, everything is that much bigger. But, I would swear the snow drifts were six foot tall. There was another lad with me in that billet and we shared a bed, which was quite common. He wet the bed so they decided to move me again. They probably thought; 'I wonder which one is leaking?' That was in Gladstone Street, the other side of Glossop.

Another Glossop billet was in Surrey Street with Mr and Mrs Horace Webster, who at that time, were childless. Their son, Ian Webster, was born after my departure from there. I met him later on at one of our reunions. I have now outlived him but I am still in contact with his widow. This was my longest stay. My education continued at the Duke of Norfolk School situated in old Glossop. I moved to Littlemore before taking the scholarship and joining the Lowestoft Grammar School group, in Worksop. I was billeted at no less than four places in my three years in Glossop before moving to Worksop. I was always treated well.

Again, I have no memories of the Glossop to Worksop journey, nor who met me and allocated me somewhere to stay. By this time I would have been eleven.

Worksop was memorable for sharing the Central School buildings. Assembly was alternately 9.00am or 9.15am. The Central School went in at 9.00am and the evacuated grammar school at 9.15am and the next week it was switched round. On my first day, I was 15 mins early arriving at 9.00am, on a 9.15am week! I had my black and red school cap on and when I turned up at school I couldn't see anyone with a cap the same as mine. Then the next lot came along and they all did have the same cap so I knew I must be with them. You wonder how they managed to accommodate double the number of children in the same accommodation. We also went into school on Saturday morning. We enrolled for chess or handicraft activities, ending, with a final assembly concert. That kept us out of the hair of the lady we were billeted with.

In Worksop I was billeted, first of all with Mr and Mrs Bembridge, and the second billet was with the Allertons in Victoria Road. The man was a miner who worked in the Manton Pit. He became famous for hitting the fastest number of runs for Nott's County. He kept the cricket bat there in the house.

My parents came to visit me two or three times and sent me food parcels. I must have been a little horror; a right tearaway. I was in six billets in all. I was in Glossop for two years, in four billets, and in Worksop for one year, in two billets.

I came back to Lowestoft at about Christmas 1944, just in time to experience buzz bombs or doodle bugs (V1 Flying Bombs). They switched off and then they quietly came down. Later, they were deliberately crashed, but the earlier ones just ran out of fuel. I remember one flying bomb, the one that came down in Carlton Colville, and destroyed a little chapel there.

I went to Lowestoft Grammar School and I am on the 1948/49 school picture. This was the first picture of the Grammar School taken after World War 2. I was in the Grammar School till 1948.

My career meant I was travelling all my life. I was at The Fishery's Laboratories in Lowestoft and did three trips to the Arctic. I was useless at school but I used to come top at Chemistry and bottom in everything else. Eventually, when I got enough qualifications, I went to Scotland for five years studying Chemistry. I am a graduate of the University of St Andrews and ended up in Solid Fuel Rocketry in Waltham Abbey.

Apart from a brief weekend visit to stay with the Websters, when I was at R.A.F. Padgate, I didn't return until a visit was organised by the Lowestoft Evacuee Association in 2008. I met Ian Webster then who had recently retired. I'd last seen him when he was still at school. I was introduced to his wife, Sheila, who is always welcoming to the Lowestoft Evacuees, although, sadly Ian has since died.

Chris Brooks, Founder of Lowestoft Evacuees Association, has taken photographs of the billet in Manor Park Road and also the ones in Gladstone Street and Surrey Street. When we were up there we knocked on the doors but the people were out. The second place I was at in Worksop was in Victoria Street, I have a picture of that house again taken by Chris Brooks.

Bryan on the left with Ian Webster, son of his
foster parents in Glossop

Violet (Vi) Sterry (née Mills), was twelve when she was evacuated to Whitwell, a very small village in Derbyshire, and later to Glossop. Her brother, Kenny, and sister, Olive, went to Glossop.

LIKE A CATTLE MARKET

Vi on the right of the picture

When we were at Notley Road School, we used to swap cigarette cards, saying 'ciggy a go, ciggy a go'. Once my brother said to us, 'Come with me, and I'll show you a human ape.' When I got there he got a big mirror out and showed us our own faces! I thought that was a 'swiz'. That was before we were evacuated. I was twelve, and attending Notley Road School, when I went to Whitwell. I was on my own because I went to a different school to my brother and sister. They went to Glossop with their school.

When we arrived in Whitwell, we were taken to a big hall. It was like a cattle market. People were saying, 'I'll have those two over there' or 'I'll have that one there.' Eventually all the children disappeared and there was just three of us left. Me and the twins, Vera and Eileen. One woman said, 'I'll have that one and you can have the twins.' The twins both stood there and cried. The woman asked what they were crying for. They said, 'We want to go with Vi'. Eventually, they sorted it out and allowed us three to go together. We went to Mr and Mrs Blackwell. Mr Blackwell worked down the pit. He was a lovely man. They had one daughter, Dorothy. She was about seventeen.

We went to school every day of the week, even on a Saturday and Sunday morning; only having Sunday afternoon off. I suppose it helped the people we were staying with, who were responsible for us, because it meant they knew where we were.

When we had been there a couple of months, the air-raid siren went. Mrs Blackwell told us to get under the stairs. They didn't have air-raid shelters. There was a big thud. An incendiary bomb had been dropped in the field at the back of our house.

The word went around the village that Mrs Blackwell's house had been bombed. People didn't realise it, but it had hit a big haystack in the field at the back of the house. The house had not been hit. Anyway, for a while, they all thought, *Poor Mrs Blackwell and her evacuees.* Over the years I have thought that it was amazing that to get away from bombing, I left Lowestoft, where I had not known any bombing, and went to a place where a bomb dropped behind the house I was in.

Being twins, Vera and Irene were a bit of a novelty. They were the same age as me and were my best friends. However, Mrs Blackwell would say to me, 'When you go out, just make sure they have their coats on', or if it rained, 'Make sure they have their macs.' I used to get the blame if they didn't!

My mother and father split up during the war and my mother joined the WAAF. My older brother, Robert, went into the Navy. My older sister, Barbara, also went in the WAAF. This meant my mother and father came to visit at different times. My mother visited on her seven days' leave, then my father visited on his seven days' leave. As I didn't go to school when either of them visited, it meant I had a lot of time off school! When I did go, the Head teacher would say 'Morning Stranger'. As my parents were in the forces nothing was said.

I was there about nine months when my dad decided to move me to where my sister Olive and brother Kenny were. He was having to split his leave time between two places when he visited and was spending quite a lot of time travelling between. He went to see Miss Munnings, the Headmistress, and it was agreed that I should be transferred to Glossop where Kenny and Olive were already living.

My father was in the Merchant Navy. During the war he worked in the engine room on an oil tanker taking oil into Guernsey and Jersey. They had to get out of there in a hurry because the Germans were about to occupy the Channel Isles. When he came home he always had a suit on with a peak cap with a badge. My friends thought he was an admiral!

So, I went to Glossop and went to the West End School. I knew Ivy Durrant from Lowestoft but all the others were complete strangers. The teacher that taught us wasn't a very nice teacher. He used to sit with his arm around one of the young girls in the class for a lot of the time. He wasn't bothered about teaching us. If the teacher isn't bothered, then the pupil won't be bothered.

I didn't like one of the houses I lived in. There was a son living there who was in the Navy. When he came home one time, I was playing behind a wall with a young boy. We were throwing a ball against the wall. The navy man said, 'What were you doing behind that wall?' I told him I was throwing the ball against the wall. He said, 'No you weren't. Next time I come home on leave I'll show you what you were doing.' That put the fear of God up me. After he went away I thought to myself, well, I'm going to make sure I'm not living in this house when he comes back. So when my father came I told him I didn't like living there anymore and if he didn't move me I would go back to Lowestoft and live with one of my aunties. He had me moved. In the next house there were three daughters and a son. I was happy as a 'sand-boy' there.

I was fourteen and able to leave school. My older sister, Barbara, came to Glossop to work. I told her I was going to leave school and she should get me a job with her. It was a small town and there were not many places to work. She worked in a rope factory, so that is where I went, and I liked the work. They used to say that when the war was over they would be making the rope that would fly the flag to announce we had won the war. I was paid £1 a week. I paid for my keep out of that so didn't have much left over to spend.

While I worked there I had a friend named Joan Heap. We would go the local villages to the cinema and dances. Her father was very strict and she had to make sure she was home on time or she wouldn't be able to go the next week. She was a Derbyshire person and I wrote to her for a while after I came back home.

My sister, Barbara, wrote to my Aunt Millie and asked her if she would take her in, which she did. She also wrote to another aunt, who lived in Blackheath Road, and she took me in. My parents got back together again but not until we were all grown up and married.

I didn't go back to Glossop after the war but I went to Whitwell. Things looked different after being away for a lot of years. I walked down the road and took a look at the recreation ground. I think one of the twins, Eileen, stayed in Whitwell. I believe Vera came back to Lowestoft. I met up with them later at an evacuee reunion.

Vi second row from the back, 3rd from right

Margaret Stone, (née Hall), was nine years old and attending Church Road School when she was evacuated from Lowestoft in June 1940 to Langwith in Derbyshire. She was with her sister, Kathleen, who was eighteen months older.

THIS IS YOUR ROOM, AND YOU STAY IN THERE!

Margaret on the right with her sister Kathleen

I went to Church Road School. I remember being at the railway station and feeling excited because we thought we were going out for the day. At that age, we didn't realise what was happening and had no idea that we wouldn't be coming back home. It was exciting getting into the train carriage. My aunt kept a leather goods shop at the north end of town and she gave both my sister, and I, a leather writing case. We used it to put our sandwiches in!

I'm not sure what station we arrived at, but we found ourselves in Shirebrook and there were coaches, taking children to different areas.

My sister and I were wearing our labels so they knew where to send us. We all went to a local hall and were told to sit in four rows back to back. Kath and I sat in the front near the stage. We couldn't understand why people were coming in and children were going out with them.

When people came in, they would look at the faces of the children, then pick out who they thought they would like. There were five of us left when a lady walked in. She walked past my sister and I and looked at the two children in the middle row. Then she went and looked at another child, then she came back to us two. She spoke to one of the women, who then came over and said, 'You are going with this lady.' It was like a cattle market.

She took us to her house. There are little things I can remember very clearly. She took us up to the landing, where there was a great big trunk. We later discovered it contained bags and bags of sugar, which was rationed at the time. There were two doors off the landing. She took me and my bag and she said, 'This is your room and you stay in **there**!' She then took my sister across to the other door and said, 'And this is your room and you stay in **there**!' There was no other interaction. We took our bags into our rooms and then went downstairs for a drink. There was a man who lived in the house but there were no other children.

My sister and I were not very often allowed downstairs. We had to stay in our own separate rooms. All through the stay with her, we got our own breakfast and washed up before school. We looked after ourselves in the same way in the evening. She was very strict; I don't think she really wanted us. I think she was clever, she wanted the allowance for having evacuees.

We thought that we were in a luxury house because there was a big lawn at the front and a big lawn at the back. That feeling didn't last long. They had two dogs. First thing in the morning, when we came down, we were told, 'Get your chores done.' This meant Kath went out the back, and I went out the front, and we had to clear the mess up from the dogs. That was our first job in the morning. We would then come in to have our breakfast, which didn't consist of very much.

What sticks in my mind was that I could never understand why, but she would stand in front of the fire, then turn round and face the other way, then turn back again. She would do this, holding her dress out. Of course, she was trying to get herself warm.

As things turned out, people knew what she was like. After we left her, we found out that people used to talk about her going up to the top end of the village, where the pub was, and sitting on the steps, waiting for someone to take her home. There was something going on that we were not old enough to understand. We were with her for about eight months.

There was a brook in the village and it was used as a sheep dip. Well, we stood watching the sheep and my sister slipped and fell in. We both stood there crying like anything because we daren't go back to our lodgings, to that woman. The vicar and his wife came across to us and the vicar's wife said, 'Come along, never mind, don't worry, come to the Vicarage.' She washed and dried my sister's clothes and gave her a gown to wear. It was lovely in the vicarage compared to where we were.

My mum was still in Lowestoft. My Dad was a fireman. When the library was struck by a bomb, my dad was manning the pumps outside, with the officer. A bomb had come down and dropped a few yards away from him. Fortunately, the bomb blast went upwards so it didn't touch them. However, he suffered from shock and they sent him to a fire station in the Midlands to convalesce. It was a coincidence that he came to the Midlands. So Mum came as well. She was expecting my younger sister, Christine, at the time. The lady who we were staying with wouldn't take mum in.

Across the road from where we were, there was an old farmhouse. The lady there said she would take Mum in for a while, until she had the baby. So my sister, Christine, was born there. After she had Christine, the woman said Mum would have to go and find other lodgings. She found other lodgings for us all, which, again, were not very nice. The man there used to go out and shoot rabbits and pheasants, which he shouldn't have been doing. They had two children but I don't think she knew how to wash - wash the children, wash herself, wash anything. These things stick in your mind. When I walked into the room, she would be sitting with one of the children on her knee and she would be going through their hair, looking for nits. I didn't understand what she was doing at the time.

There was an elderly couple a few doors up and they took us in while Dad was ill. In the end, Dad moved to a hospital at Mansfield and got over his illness.

Eventually, Mum and Dad had had enough and we came back to Lowestoft, in the middle of the bombing. We didn't come back to our old house. My aunt owned quite a few properties in Lowestoft. She took our house over and we had one of her houses in Maidstone Road. We came back in the worst part of the war. We saw the doodlebugs going up the river. I can remember my little sister, Christine, being about six months old, and her lying on the settee as the doodle bugs came over. We had one of those iron Morrison's Shelters in the middle of the room, which we used as a table. Later, we had an air-raid shelter put in at the bottom of the garden and we used to sleep in there. When we got back, Kath and I went to the only school that was open. It was in Kirkley Run. We walked there from Maidstone Road, which was quite a long way.

It was so very much to happen to a young person in such a short time. It made me more independent because when you don't have your parents around there is no one close enough to ask and you have to work things out for yourself. I can't say that we were unfortunate. Some other children had a terrible time.

My husband Ted's mother wouldn't allow him to be evacuated. There were four of them and, as most of the schools were closed, they all went to a private school in Oulton Broad with a lady called Mrs Baker. He stayed there until Pakefield School opened again. He then helped his father paint the boats at Richards Shipyard. I met him when we both went to social evenings and I would tell him which records I wanted played. We got married and have two daughters and a son. One daughter lives in Vancouver and our son lives in Toronto. Our other daughter lives nearby in Kessingland.

We went back to Langwith a couple of times with the Lowestoft Evacuee Association. Most of the people who had been there had moved. We remembered the school. To get to school we would cross the road and go through a wood. It was quite good in the summertime, but not walking through the wood, with all those trees, in the dark in the winter.

Margaret after the war

Ernie Martin was one of twelve children. He was eight years old when he was evacuated to Derbyshire in June 1940, with three of his siblings, Jessie, Pauline and Ivan.

OUR SCHOOL WAS HEAVILY BOMBED
Ernie Martin 1931 – 2020

Ernie and Pauline

I went to Wilde's Score School, which took a direct hit during the war. On Evacuation day the coaches lined up along Whapload Road, adjacent to Wilde's Score, took us to the station and away we went.

There were three villages in one: Bramley Vale, Doe Lea, and Glapwell. That's where Ivan, Pauline and I went. Because she was older, our sister Jessie went to a different school and therefore went with her school to Shirebook six miles away.

First Billet

The first billet was in Bramley Vale. I was with my young sister, Pauline. Then, I was moved to somewhere else and I had to leave her behind. People didn't really want me. Sometimes they found us children too much of a handful and so we were moved on.

Second Billet

At the second billet, at Doe Lea, again, they were not interested in having any extra children. How long I was there I don't know.

Third Billet

This billet, also at Doe Lea, was a lucky one. I was with Mr and Mrs Gould and that is where I stayed for the rest of the time. I was very happy there. They were good people - very, very fair. I did all my chores, you accepted that, chopping wood and getting the coal in. The pit families got a ton of coal a month free. They would bring it in a lorry and dump it outside the back door, then we would shovel it into the coalhouse. This meant that they didn't need to worry about putting a spade full of coal on the fire! There was plenty. If they didn't take a ton of coal they were paid £5.

What I couldn't understand was, when they tipped the cinders away at the pit, some of them were still alight. It was wartime, and in the dark, you could see the ashes glowing a mile away. I couldn't fathom that out.

Mr Gould worked down the pit splicing and renewing various cables. He was a good lad, he worked eight to twelve hours, seven days a week. He would come up from the pit, have his beer before his dinner, and then have his sleep. You never had any problems with him being drunk or anything. A man amongst men.

Our school was about two and a half miles away and we had to go over five fields to get there. Five miles a day whatever the weather. The second day we were there, at the last stile we had to go over, there were two or three local boys blocking our way. Mr brother, Ivan, got hold of the one doing all of the 'mouthing' and sorted him out. They let us through and after that we didn't have any trouble with the local boys and we even 'palled up' with some of them.

It was pitch black in the villages during the war. No lights. The things we used to get up to you would never believe. We would pinch people's clothes lines, lash them across the road to another house, pull them tight, and bang on the doors. When they went to open the door, it wouldn't open. Nobody ever caught us because they couldn't get out of the doors.

One day we were at the top of the village playing around and this kid came charging down the road and said, 'Look what I've got.' He had a hand grenade! He looked at it, pulled it, and blue smoke started coming out. He threw it and it blew up. A piece of shrapnel went through a window and just missed a picture on a lady's wall. We were very lucky nobody got hurt.

I remember a plane came over and dropped a bomb intended for the Sheffield raid. It killed two cows. The Pilot must have been lost or something and he just pulled the plug and dropped the bomb.

We were adjacent to an air force parachute training camp in Hardwick Hall in Chesterfield. We used to have a laugh with them. We often watched them route marching. In the snow, as they were marching, we would throw snowballs at them. They couldn't do anything could they! But one day the Sergeant dismissed them on the march and they chased after us and stuck snow down the back of our neck and all sorts. We lost the battle that day.

It was a Saturday afternoon and I went to the Co-op shop at the end of the village to get a loaf of bread. This here fella came walking towards me. When I saw him I stopped and just stood there mesmerized. I didn't know what to make of it. He said, 'Excuse me, can you tell me what time the buses run to Mansfield?' It was my Dad! He had come up to see us. He knew who I was. He said, 'Do you know who I am?' I told him I did. He stayed for the weekend. That was the last time I ever saw him. He died of cancer in 1944. I think he was sixty-three. He was twenty-two years in the navy and a naval pensioner. Before the war he got an award for saving an engineer's life when he was in the navy in Weihaiwei in China. He worked on the Lowestoft coastguard station as a lookout. When the war started they issued them with rifles. If the Germans had invaded they wouldn't have got far with my father there!

I suppose he knew he was dying and that is why he came to see us. That was when I came back home to Lowestoft, to the funeral. We came back by train. We didn't know our school had been bombed till we got home. I then went to Notley Road School and finished my schooling at Church Road School. In 1945, when the war finished, most of the children were speaking with a Derbyshire accent. I was happy to be back because my ambition was to be a Navy man or seaman and when I got back to Lowestoft there were plenty of ships.

I kept in touch with Mr and Mrs Gould and their daughter Barbara. When I got older I went back and had a pint with him in the boozer. I went down the pit when I was on leave one time. Mr Gould's son, Michael, took me down. It wasn't a very deep one, but deep enough, at 1200 ft!

Mr and Mrs Gould came to Lowestoft to visit a couple of times. I have been back up there dozens of times since the war and am still in touch with their daughter on-line. I always looked forward to seeing him.

Most of the work I did was wire splicing with the fishing fleet after the war. It was hard on the hands. After splicing all day I would be picking pieces of wire out of my fingers, digging and digging till the pain disappeared. Then modernisation stepped in and we got ferrule which could, instead of doing two an hour, did thirty by machine. The other place I did wire splicing was in the Cameroon in Central Africa.

I met my wife, Doreen, when I was on leave from the Merchant Navy. She was selling ice-creams at Capaldi's in Bevan Street, Lowestoft.

Being evacuated was a good experience and a very important part of my life. I saw things I would never have otherwise seen. I loved the countryside, we would be out all day in the woods eating nuts.

I have been to most of the Lowestoft Evacuee Association reunions.

I sometimes think about the futility of man and ask myself whether it was worth all those millions of lives?

Ernie on the left with other members of his family

Eric Thompson was five years old and living in Gorleston when he was evacuated to Bircotes near Doncaster. He is the husband of Rona Thompson, an evacuee from Lowestoft and whose story also appears in this book.

I HAD NEVER EVEN BEEN ON A BUS!

Eric centre with brothers Gordon and Arnold

I was five years old and just starting school at the Alderman Leech School in Gorleston when I was evacuated to Bircotes, a small mining village not far from Doncaster. I had an older brother, Arnold, who was two and a half years older than me. I also had a younger brother, Gordon, and sister Irene, who were not old enough to be evacuated. I had never been away before. I had never even been on a bus.

Arnold had been at school for a while and I had just started school. All I can remember about the day we were evacuated is that we got a train from Great Yarmouth to Doncaster and I was sick all the way. There must have been a bus meet us at the other end that took us to Bircotes, about ten to twelve miles south of Doncaster.

I can remember walking with my brother, two by two crocodile style through the village. There was a woman teacher at the front of the line and someone at the back. I had my case, gas mask, and a label round my neck. I remember the crocodile line stopping and the woman teacher coming to speak to my older brother, Arnold. He was the brain of the family, the 'Jewel in the Crown'. She came up to him and said, 'The two of you go to that lady she is expecting you.' The lady was standing on her path leaning on the front gate. My brother, not being very pleased about being lumbered with a younger sibling, especially one who had been sick all the way on the train, said, 'I don't want to be with *him*.' But we had to go with her.

So, we were billeted with Mr and Mrs Calvert. Mr Calvert worked down the pit. Everybody in the village lived in a pit house. It was a perk of working at the pit. People didn't have cars so everybody needed to live close to the coal mine.

Mother didn't like the idea of the family being split up and she was the driving force of our parents. She had been writing letters to the people we were evacuated with and found out that if you got a job at the colliery it entitled you to a rented house in the village. It was called Harworth Colliery. Father, who was a milkman, got a job as a surface worker at Harworth Colliery which then entitled him to a rented house. I can't remember how long it was before mother and father moved into the village but the house we were allocated was only a couple of hundred yards away from where we boys had been living as evacuees. So we boys vacated Mr and Mrs Calvert's house and moved in with mother and father.

The people next door had only moved into their pit house the day before. They were of mining stock from the Newcastle area. It was hilarious because my mother spoke 'Silly Suffolk' and had a broad accent. The Geordie's mother, next door, couldn't understand 'Silly Suffolk', and we couldn't understand her.

Father was too old to be 'called up' but he wasn't very happy in the job at the pit so he volunteered for the RAF. However we continued to live in the pit house. People were very kind I remember them saying, 'can we bring you some coal?' The miners' families got a free coal allowance. We stayed in the pit house while my father joined the RAF. I'm sure the colliery would have rather he continued to work at the pit!

We went to the village school and during the last year I was head boy. When we left in 1949 I was aged fourteen. I was the only male in the village who didn't go down the pit. There never seemed to be any discussion about where they would work when they left school. You left school on the Friday and were expected to start down the pit on the Monday and it was the best paid job you could get.

I was determined that I was not going to live the life of a mole down the pit so I decided that I must get a trade. At school there was no employment advice but I got an apprenticeship with British Rail. It meant me travelling twelve miles to work in Doncaster. There were thousands of people working there and, from day one, you were put on piecework. Looking back it was cheap labour but it was a good apprenticeship and I served my time.

After father was de-mobbed, for us to live in that house he had to work at the pit. So he went back to the pit. Our parents both stayed in the colliery house until father died when he was early to mid-fifties. By then it was well after the war (1955) and we had been up there at least fifteen years and I was about twenty. Mother was in her late forties. In those days when the husband died and the wife was under fifty that made her a pensioning widow. If she had been a bit older and been over fifty she would have had a pension of about £2.10 shillings per week but as she was under fifty she got 10 shillings and paid 7 shillings and 6 pence out of that for rent.

Eventually I applied for and got a job in the merchant navy as an engineer. I had my 21st birthday in New Zealand. I met Rona, my wife, when I was about twenty seven. She came from Lowestoft and we met at to the Floral Hall in Gorleston and finally got married in 1965 when I was thirty. We only saw a little of each other as I was away at sea most of the time, but we were very happy.

I can't remember how we discovered we had both been evacuated, but when we went up to Scotland or Lakeside we would make a detour to go back to see Bircotes.

Eric on the left with his two brothers and sister Irene

Rona Thompson, (née Jacques), was eleven years old and attending Church Road Junior School, when she was evacuated from Lowestoft, on 2nd June 1940, to Hillstown, a small village near Chesterfield.

THE OLDER CHILDREN WOULD TEACH

Rona front row second from the right with The Norfolk Skipping Team

I was eleven, and the youngest of four sisters, when I was evacuated. When we left Lowestoft, our parents made sure we had our labels on and our gas masks. We liked to see who had the best cover for the gas mask. The sandwiches we were given were all gone well before we got to Lowestoft station.

It had been decided that all the class would go to Hillstown. I was with Jean Gower who I am still in touch with. Unfortunately the lady we were to be billeted with had already got one evacuee and she only wanted two. So Jean and I were split up. However, I did see her while we were there. I was in the same billet as another girl called Jean. I haven't heard from her for a long, long time.

Jean and I were at the local school for a short time. Mr Bull was the only teacher from our school to come with us. There were not enough teachers to cope with the number of children and give us the education we needed. Therefore, we older children would teach the younger ones to read.

While we were at this school the results came through for the scholarship, which we had taken before we left home. We had passed the scholarship. There was a Grammar school there called The Denes School. They told us they would send us, the children who had already passed to go to a grammar school, to The Denes School. But they never did. Eventually, they sent us to the National School at Bolsover. Unfortunately, when we got there, they had been studying America and we knew nothing at all about it. So they gave us average marks for that. Once settled in their classes, I never came any lower than twelfth, so I think I did quite well. We had a lovely teacher there called Mr Baker (from Lowestoft) who always made sure there were stamps and writing pads for us to write home.

Our billet was a very good one. The husband was a miner and a fireman when there were air raids. I shared a room with Jean and I remember, when strawberries were in season, our foster mother would make us strawberry pie every Monday lunchtime. Our foster parents weren't church people but they were good people and we always went to Sunday school.

They didn't have any children of their own, but while we were there, one night there was a lot of crying and the next day a baby appeared. We didn't know where it came from. I don't think it was their child. We never did find out. The baby stayed in the house for a while then it vanished as suddenly as it came.

I played with the local children and I was taken to visit relations of our foster parents. I remember sleeping top and tail and that these relations had a sweet shop. It was a rarity to have sweets during the war as they were on ration, but being a sweet shop they always had plenty.

It was an important time in our education and Jean's parents wanted her to go to private school so she went to Retford. When she was getting ready to leave I started to feel I wanted to go home. Her private school hadn't started and so when her mother came to fetch her she brought me home as well. We travelled by train. I was away for about four months.

A short time after I got home a letter came for my mother from the foster mother I had been billeted with. It said what an ungrateful girl I was. This was because while I was still there, and homesick, I had written a letter to my mother which said the lady was very good but was not very 'particular'. I was saying that the house wasn't clean. I must have left it in my cupboard and the lady had found it. The house wasn't really dirty, it was very clean. I just made it up because I wanted to give my mother a reason to let me come home. My mother made me write a letter back to say I was homesick and I would not normally have said that. After I had made an apology, I heard from her often and we kept in touch for years. Suddenly the letters stopped in 1969 and I assumed she had passed on. My mother wasn't very well off, so, I never went back to Hillstown.

When I got back to Lowestoft, where the Lowestoft College is now, there was a big field nearby where we used to play. A bomb was dropped on it. Three horses were in the field at the time and they were all killed. I lived in Princes Road, which backed onto that field and the roof of our house came in. I've always been a bit hard of hearing and I shared a room with my two sisters Connie and Zenda. I was the youngest, I had a single bed, and they had a double bed. When there was an air raid they used to shout to me 'get under the bed'. I couldn't hear them, so they were well under the bed on this occasion, before I even realised what was happening.

My father, my mother's second husband, had been a professional musician. He wrote music, played the violin, and conducted the score of many silent films, including Romona and the Prisoner of Zenda, after which my sister and I are named. Although my name is Romona, I am known as Rona. He also played in the orchestra pit at silent films.

My sister Zenda was three years older than me and next in age. Zenda wasn't evacuated. She was a dancer. She was thirteen and, as you left school at fourteen, it hadn't seemed worth her going. I remember her going away as a dancer to a place where there was a lot of army personnel. She was with Randolph Sutton who ran variety shows and was sometimes on the radio at that time. My brother in law, my oldest sister's husband, heard that the show was somewhere where there was lots of enemy activity so he went and brought her back home.

At age thirteen, I got a job as a cashier bookkeeper in a butcher's shop. I was going to school part time and working part time. I used to go to work at 8.30am until 10.00am then cycled to school for 10.30am. At noon I cycled home to lunch then back to school 1.30pm to 3.00 pm. Then I went to work until 5 pm.

I met my husband Eric at the Floral Hall in Gorleston. I joined a dance skipping group 'The Norfolk Skipping Team' winning a national competition and was invited to perform at the Royal Albert Hall, which we did. I went on performing until I was seventy-five. I have attended Lowestoft Evacuee Reunions four or five times.

Rona appearing at the Royal Albert Hall

Gordon Sewell was eight years old and his brother, Ernest, was ten when they were evacuated from Lowestoft to Glossop in Derbyshire in June 1940. He lived in Ontario Road, Lowestoft and attended Lovewell Road School.

I'LL HAVE *HIM!*

Lovewell Road Boy's School while evacuated to Glossop.
Gordon back row 5th from the right wearing braces.

I was 'carted' around Glossop, with all the other evacuees to find a billet. The lady who took us only wanted to take one child, but my mother had told us that we, whatever happened, would not be parted. My brother was a year and four months older than me, but I was the bossy one. The lady said, 'I'll have **him**', which was me. I was a cute little kid with curly hair in those days. I grabbed my brother's hand and said, 'We will not be parted'. She had to take somebody, it was the law, so she decided to take the two of us. Thereby, after that, she resented the fact that she had two and from then on was an 'old harridan'. Her husband had died. Her house was almost empty. That is how she lived her life. Looking at it now, with a career in psychology behind me, I realise that she was a very unhappy woman.

I shared a bed with my brother. We were fed adequately, bearing in mind it was wartime and there was rationing. I couldn't compare it to the way my mother kept us but then the circumstances were different. Of course, foster parents received an allowance for our keep.

At Christmas time, we were told to write to our mother and say we needed a new pair of rubber boots and new undervests. My mother was astute enough to know that there was no way Gordon would want a pair of rubber boots for Christmas. He would want a toy train or a car. So, my mother saw through it. What kind of eight year old is going to ask for a new undervest for Christmas? But the lady dictated the letters. I was always aware (not totally consciously) that we, as a team, were unwanted in this house. I was the one she wanted to take in. However, my brother was no trouble at all, she should have wanted him not me.

Most of the children of the same age as us went to the same school in Glossop. Ernest and I were in different classes in school of course, therefore our lives were separated during the classroom time. My brother was not a particularly gregarious person so he didn't make friends easily, but those friends he did make lasted his lifetime. I was always gregarious and a daredevil.

There were some brothers who lived near us in Ontario Road, Lowestoft who were evacuated to Glossop too. The lady in Glossop who took them took eight kids in. She also had two or three of her own. They had a whale of a time. We envied them because, in that house, it was all rough and tumble. They were in clover. However, many foster parents didn't want the children they had taken in and some, after a while, realised it wasn't just for a week!

My evacuation with foster parents was somewhat short lived because my mother could tell that things were not as they should be. She wasn't going to put up with that, so she decided to move to Glossop and take us out of our billet. We were in our billet for two years before she came to Glossop and rented a house not too far away from where we were living. She then realised she was pregnant. My younger brother was born in a nursing home while we lived in that house. We stayed at the same school in Glossop and became a family again. We had a long walk to school past a paper mill. There was a stream running by and there was an absolutely putrid smell from there. I remember that clearly. It was like a mixture of dandelion, burdock, and sarsaparilla.

I got up to any mischief that was possible. I led my brother into things and I was always being cuffed around the head for something I had done. I don't remember any of the boys in Glossop but there was one girl who lived nearby. We played with her, for the first few months we were there, in nearby fields. Unfortunately, she caught diphtheria and died. Her name was Dorothy and she was the best friend we had up there. There were several children from Lowestoft billeted around the area and we saw them frequently. One of the girls became a Nursing Sister at Lowestoft Hospital. I later trained as a nurse and eventually also took over that role.

My father was on leave and visiting us one time. He and my mother were on a bus in Glossop. The people who were sitting, either in front or behind them, started talking about bombings in Lowestoft and about a house in Ontario Road that had been ransacked. It turned out to be my mother and father's house. They learnt about it on top of a bus in Glossop.

For years, I had a very bad impediment of my speech. I couldn't even go into a shop and ask for a box of matches. When back from Derbyshire, I went to Bungay Area School. The Headmaster there caught me, one day, walking around with a Charles Dickens book. He said, 'Are you reading that Gordon?' I said, 'Yes Sir.' He gave me a pat on the head. Several weeks later, he came out to the bicycle shed and asked 'What are you doing here, Gordon?' I couldn't say, 'I am waiting for my brother'. I couldn't get the words out and was trying to avoid speaking. From that moment, his opinion of me completely changed. He thought I was a 'dullard'. I was nineteen before I got control of the speech impediment. My experience of being an evacuee may have added to it. I don't recall the impediment in the years before being evacuated. I had left everything that was familiar and there was no love in the house I was in. I realised years later that it was a handicap in my future.

When I was in the Air Force in Egypt, I took a part time job with the broadcasting service. We had to close every night with, '*And so we have come to the end of our broadcasting for today. We shall be with you tomorrow morning, at 06.00 hours. Until then, we wish you a very good night. Good night everybody.*' I knew that when it came to 'we shall' it could be a problem for me so I would change it to '*we will be with you again tomorrow morning*' which I knew would be no problem for me. I got a note from the Controller to say I didn't close down correctly. They never knew the reason why.

However, when I was working at Edgeware Hospital, a speech therapist and I were talking about impediments. I told her that, I myself had a very bad speech impediment. She said, 'I don't believe you Gordon'. This meant I had learnt to control it.

I did my psychiatric nursing first, then my general nursing. I then saw an advertisement for Nursing Officers At Sea with the Blue Funnel Line, so I applied and was appointed. It was a wonderful job and I loved every moment of it. After I left I went to Saudi Arabia in 1969, originally for three years, but stayed for twenty three years.

During that time, I helped to set up two hospitals and eight medical centres across the Kingdom and met a number of prominent people including a Crown Prince who became King Abdullah.

Looking back on my evacuation experience and now, with my psychiatric training, I realise that evacuees were really displaced persons but despite this, certainly in my case, I came through it a stronger person.

Gordon on the right aboard Empire Windrush on the way to his posting in Egypt while in the Royal Air Force.

Rita Walpole, (née Smith), was evacuated from Lowestoft to Glossop in June 1940, and then later to Whitwell and Worksop. Her sister Gladys, who was thirteen, went to Whitwell.

SCHOLARSHIP COMPLICATIONS

Rita on the right with her friend Daphne

I was ten years old when my sister Gladys, who was thirteen, and I were evacuated. Our mother asked whether we would be kept together and was told yes. However, we went with our own school so I was with my own classmates and teachers from Lovewell Road School. Gladys went with Notley Road School. This meant that Gladys went to Whitwell and I went to Glossop. Having us in two different places made things complicated for Mum and Dad and meant they had to send two food parcels.

The day we left, I can remember going to Lovewell Road School with my dad. Mother went to Notley Road School with Gladys. Dad sat in the classroom while they got things organised. Once I saw my friend, Daphne, I wasn't bothered about what was happening. Dad had his bike with him and he rode on it behind the bus to the railway station so he could see us leave. Parents weren't allowed on the platform.

The journey was hot and we were all thirsty. Our bottles were refilled with water at the station stops. Our case was little so we only took what was necessary. Wearing our coats and hats, despite the hot day, was a way of taking more clothes. The trains were the old- fashioned ones with no corridors. This meant it was not possible for the teachers to be in every carriage.

Glossop

On arrival in Glossop, I remember thinking how strange it was because everyone had accents that I hadn't heard before.

I had two friends, Daphne and Betty. We stuck together until we were 'picked out'. When we left the hall, parties of us were taken in different directions. Daphne, Betty and I kept moving to the back hoping not to get picked. Eventually, Betty was left at a billet on her own and it was just Daphne and I. We went up, and up, and up Haig Street and were eventually left with Mr and Mrs Doyle.

Mrs Doyle had been a school teacher and Mr Doyle was the manager of the Co-op shop. He was an Alderman and had been Mayor. We were shown a picture of him as Mayor with his chain, which was made of threepenny pieces. They looked after us well. They clothed us and wrote to Mum and Dad to assure them I was happy and encouraged me to write home. I was there eighteen months. Mum and Dad had a letter from Mrs Doyle asking whether they could adopt me. My parents said 'no way'. Now I've had children of my own, I know how Mum felt. I could not have parted with my children.

Daphne, like me, took the scholarship exam at Glossop. However, our billet was located a long way from the school which the other Lowestoft children were attending. This led to our completed scholarship papers being lost and not getting to Lowestoft in time. So we never went to the Grammar school and had to go to another school, in Glossop.

Daphne's sister was older than her and was evacuated with The Central School in Lowestoft. Her sister was old enough to leave school at Christmas 1941 and was going home at the end of term. Daphne's mother said Daphne could go home with her, just for Christmas. Of course, I then also wanted to go home for Christmas, which I did.

Daphne's dad came round the day before we were to go back to Glossop and told us Daphne was in tears and wasn't going back. So, of course, I burst into tears and said I wasn't going back on my own.

Whitwell

My parents worried about my oldest sister, Elsie, being in danger, as she was working on the Lowestoft seafront. So Mum went to Whitwell, where my sister Gladys was, and took Elsie with her. Elsie got a job and worked there. After a while, Mum came home again and left Elsie and Gladys in Whitwell. I was still at home in Lowestoft. They asked if I could go there and stay with them at their billet with Mr and Mrs Horn. So I left again, to Whitwell, and we three sisters were together for a very short time.

At Whitwell School it was all Lowestoft children in one room at the Miners' Welfare Centre together with Notley Road School teachers. It was really strange for me because the boys and girls were mixed and I hadn't been used to that. I always remember the first day the Headmaster took us in. He said, 'I'm going to take you through into the hall, where they are doing Country Dancing.' We went in and the boys were doing a sword dance!

As my sister Elsie was working, she had some money and saw to my clothes. Mum used to fit me out with clothes when I went home on holiday. Dad used to give me 10 shillings and say that it was to get things I needed, like my shoes repaired.

When I was in Whitwell I had to take the scholarship exam again and because I passed to go to a grammar school that meant I couldn't continue to live at Whitwell. I needed a billet in Worksop. Therefore, I had to move away from my sisters.

Worksop

My friend Daphne had taken the scholarship again in Lowestoft and passed to go to the Grammar school. At this time, her parents decided she would be better off, what with all the bombing in Lowestoft, to go away again. She was evacuated again, this time to Worksop. She was with Mr and Mrs Pepper and they agreed to take me also.

167

Mr and Mrs Pepper were good people. However, by this time I was reaching the end of my 'strength'. Mr Pepper used to get up and cook us a breakfast on Sunday, otherwise we used to get up and get ourselves off to school. Mrs Pepper kept in touch after the war, she wrote to my mother.

As Daphne's dad, Mr Bunn, had a fish stall, he used to send fish and all sorts of things for Daphne. I used to love it when Daphne got her box, as we used to share. She got more than me because Mum and Dad had two parcels to send.

During all this time, I would sometimes come home for holidays. Mum and Dad were fire wardens. If I came home and both Mum and Dad were on duty, I wouldn't be able to be at home on my own. Even if Mother was at home she could have been called out. So I would be taken to my grandad's and I used to sleep in Grandad's shelter.

Dad was working on the docks and the sea defences at this time. Later, when I went to that area, I would remember how he said he used to see the German planes come in with their machine guns, and how he would jump onto the rocks.

When they told us we were going home for good, we all cheered and hugged each other. We sang on the way home in the train. When we were all back in Lowestoft again, some of Mrs Horn's grandchildren come from Whitwell to see us.

I eventually went to Lowestoft Grammar school at age twelve. When I left school, at sixteen, my first job was in a solicitor's office. After that, I went to work in the office at the Eastern Coach Works. I met my husband, Kenneth, at the Palais de Dance in Lowestoft. Kenneth played for Lowestoft Town Football team and also played cricket.

Rita front row on the right with her sister Gladys front row left

Kathleen Wilton was eight years old and attending Roman Hill Junior School when she was evacuated from Lowestoft to Creswell in Derbyshire with her little brother, Edwin aged six. Her older brother Paul was twelve and went to Clowne.

THEIR FALSE TEETH WOULD DROP OUT!

Kathleen back row on the left

Before I was evacuated I can remember mother taking me to the Claremont Pier in Lowestoft at the beginning of September 1939 to see the boat carrying evacuees coming in from Dagenham. In fact the reason we were there was to meet my mother's cousin, Alice, with her three-week old baby, Grace. As the boat drew in to dock, I remember seeing lots of children on the deck.

I was eight when I was evacuated. My birthday was the last day of May and we went on 2 June. I had a doll for my birthday. I had several dolls but this doll was dressed in a military nurse's uniform, so she had a connection to the war. It must have broken my mother's heart to have three children evacuated.

I remember before we went, Mr Walter Howard, who lived opposite us in Wollaston Road, near the football ground, gave us each a whole bar of traveller's chocolate. We had never had a whole bar before and we were under strict instructions not to eat it all at once.

We were told about evacuation through various letters and forms. My older brother was at Roman Hill Seniors, I was at Roman Hill Juniors, and Edwin, the little one, was at Roman Hill Infants. We got up early and Dad went with Paul to the Senior School and Mum came with me and little Edwin. As instructed our parents said goodbye in the school playground. They then charged down to the railway station to see us leave.

Some children had never been in a train, so it was very exciting for them. My mother came from London and my grandma was in London so we had been there on the train. We had been on trains that had ordinary carriages but this one, taking us to Derbyshire, had tables. I had never seen a train with tables before.

When we got there, we were separated from my brother Paul, who went to a different village, Clowne. I was with my friends from the junior school. There were about thirty of us in the class. When we arrived, we went by bus to the Creswell Regors Cinema. It was there that we were allocated to foster parents. I remember they looked at our tummies. I suppose it was to see if we had any spots or any infections. Postcards were given to our foster parents to fill in with their address, to be sent back to our parents.

A lady called Margaret came, and she took me home with her. It turned out that she was the daughter of Mr and Mrs Bennett, my foster parents, the people who kept the village shop in Elmton Road. They seemed frightfully old to me but I don't suppose they were. It was wonderful. Behind the shop there was a sitting room and a kitchen. When I went in, on the table there were some chocolate biscuits. Well, I don't think we had ever had chocolate biscuits. The main thing I remember was that these chocolate biscuits were on a china plate, with an intricate pierced pattern. That was very, very special. I was then taken upstairs to my own room.

Mr Bennett seemed very old and whiskery. It turned out that he absolutely adored having a child in the house, he was lovely. He had a nice garden at the back with vegetables and flowers and there was a pigsty. Beside the pigsty, there was a little building where he cooked up all the swill for the pigs. I remember seeing the steam going up from the chimney. People would bring him left-over vegetables and things for the pigs.

Mr Bennet was very inventive. The winter of 1940 was really memorable for its cold and snow. At Christmas it snowed and snowed and snowed. A snowplough came down the main road in the village. When we went from where we lived, down to the school, the snowplough had made a passageway through the snow. The sides were far above our heads. An absolute memory.

Mr Bennet, having had a little girl of his own, knew what little girls liked. He made me an igloo with blocks of snow and ice. There was a little door just big enough for me to get in. I could take things in and he could just about look in the door. Then of course, in the summer time the garden was lovely.

I enjoyed being with them. Margaret, who must have been in her 20s, had a gentleman friend, Percival, who then became her fiancé. I was going to be at the wedding and they bought me a little blue taffeta dress, all very smart, and some black patent shoes. But Margaret decided she wanted to join the ATS, the women's army and they broke the relationship off. I didn't ever get to wear those clothes for such an event but I wore them on Sundays. I remember Percival used to come to tea on Sundays and I, wishing to say how lovely the cake Mrs Bennett had made was, and wishing to congratulate her, said, 'Oh I can see that this cake was made by Mrs Bennett,' and I produced a grey hair. The grey hair was obviously hers as she had baked the cake. I was told off for that.

At first we went to the school at the bottom of the village then we moved up to one in the middle of the village. I think they really taught us well. The local library used to bring books and I did do a lot of reading. I just loved it. We shared the playground with the local children. Many children were billeted with families who went to the local Chapels on Sundays. My mother had written to the people I was staying with and told them we were a Catholic family, so I went to the Catholic Church down at the bottom of the village near the Crags. The Chapels used to have what they called an 'anniversary', I suppose, of the foundation of their particular chapel. They had an anniversary party and they all had to learn a poem or sing a song. As my family was a Catholic family, I didn't go to any of those chapel events. I felt a bit left out.

Mr and Mrs Bennet had a covered area by the side of their shop that would have been used for a horse and cart. It was empty and we were allowed to play in there and performed concerts for each other. When I was at the village shop, everyone thought, when the sweets came in, I had lots of sweets, but I didn't. The other children all queued up and used up all the sweets. I never had any. The Bennetts had a relative in the countryside and we used to go for long walks on Sundays. I remember the fields of big white daisies.

My grandma in London became ill. My mother wanted the three of us children to go and see her. She discovered somehow that Mr Orchard, one of the teachers, was taking his family by train to London. I don't know how she found this out, but she asked him if he would mind looking after the three of us on the train and we would be met at Liverpool Street. So we went to London and were taken to see Grandma. She was lying in bed in her front room with a white crochet counterpane, a lace edged pillow and a lace edged nightdress collar. Lying there, her face was as white as all these things. She said she would see us in the morning. In the morning my auntie Nan said Grandma has gone to heaven. They said she had been waiting to see us.

On the day of the funeral, we three went over the road to a lady who had a corner house that had been a shop and had a balcony. We were able to stand on the balcony and watch the funeral from there. There were black horses with lovely feathers and all the old-fashioned things to do with funerals. This lady used to have a cow some years before. Aunt Rose used to say if someone had done something stupid, this lady would say, 'You are as daft as my cow Betty'.

When Margaret went into the ATS her elderly parents weren't able to look after me, so I went to a different dwelling, with Mr and Mrs Comer. Mr and Mrs Comer lived in a different part of the village and kept a fish and chip shop. They didn't have any children but he had a twin brother. I suppose they were in their sixties. They seemed ancient to me. The twin brother used to come on Sundays and after dinner the two men would sit in the living room either side of the fire. I would be at the table with my books and crayons. Mrs Comer would go upstairs to have a rest. So there I was with these two elderly gentlemen and they would both fall asleep. I absolutely dreaded it because I knew that at any moment they would open their mouths and their false teeth would drop out!

Mrs Comer had a sister who had a dressmaking business in a house near the colliery. She used to have me in on Saturday mornings to pick up the pins. I would get sixpence for that. Mrs Bennett's sister had two daughters and she altered the dresses they had grown out of for me.

Occasionally, we would hear that the families of some of the evacuee children had been bombed back in Lowestoft. I remember one girl's mother was killed. That was very sad. We were sheltered from what was happening.

My dad went into the army. He was forty so he didn't have to go but volunteered and went into the army catering corps. When he was on leave, he came to Creswell to see us and my mum came too. I had never seen a grown-up cry, and my mother was in tears because he was going away. Later after my dad had been invalided out of the army he was on fire watch on a roof. They had a stirrup pump and a bucket of water. We had some bombing near Woolaston Road where we lived. It was quite dangerous in Lowestoft at that time.

We were kept separated from the local children. It was a mining village so a lot of the families were miners' families. There was a big recreation ground near the mine and a social club. A fair used to come each year and I remember climbing on the lorries and the equipment, jumping off and hurting my ankle. Knowing I wasn't supposed to be up there, I tried to hide it. We used to do country dancing and play cricket. That stood me in good stead later. I used to help to score the cricket matches at Somerleyton. Later, when I was at university in Birmingham, they needed someone to take a place in the women's cricket team. So, I was taken off to play in the university cricket team. I wasn't out, the innings finished, so I didn't disgrace the team.

My elder brother Paul and another boy went to Clowne. He was billeted to a man who had a small-holding. Unfortunately they didn't have a very good time because they were made to do a lot of heavy work. They would have been about twelve. Little Edwin did not have a good second billet. I only saw him at school when our classes lined up in the playground. It seemed that the clothes he had been given had been taken away and been replaced by old ones. He didn't look very well cared for.

Below is a transcript of one of Kathleen's letters home.

"10 Duke Street Creswell nr Worksop Notts. 19th May 1943

Dear Mum,

Thank-you for your letter, and money.

It is very hot at Creswell. Next Tuesday we are going to the Swimming Baths.

We were to go last Tuesday but Mr. Orchard sad that the water was too cold but will probably be warmer next week.

I am wearing my blouses now. Miss Higgins had given me two of her summer frocks which she had when she went to school. Mrs. Comer has altered them so that they look like new. At school we write letters to America. The children of America formed a society called 'The Junior Red Cross'. In that society the children send gifts to evacuees. At Christmas we had some nice presents from them.

I have just been talking to my friend Thelma. She sits just behind me at school. Tonight I have been playing with Ivy Langley and Janet Fretwell on the Fox Green. On Sunday I went to Southgate Church with Mrs. Comer.

I must close now. Mrs. Comer sends her kind regards and hopes that you are getting better.

Your loving daughter

Kathleen,

XXXXXXX"

We were there till everyone came home, by which time, the scholarship results were out and I had passed. I was due to go to Worksop to the secondary school. However, being a Catholic family my mother had other ideas and she spoke to Father Philips and between them they hatched a plan that I wasn't going with my friends to Worksop, I was going to Notre Dame in Norwich. It was still war time. I was billeted in Norwich. I didn't like it very much there. I had been spoilt as an evacuee.

After returning home, I went to university in Birmingham to study a language degree and then became a teacher in French and Latin. After 10 years teaching in Middlesex, I taught at St Mary's Catholic School in Lowestoft.

Some children had much worse experiences than I had. I was very fortunate with the families I went to. I was well looked after and interesting things happened.

Kathleen left, as Head Girl at Notre Dame High School back in Norwich

Neville Skinner's parents arranged privately for him and his brother, Barry, to be evacuated from Lowestoft to Leicester in June 1940. Neville was ten and Barry was eight. Neville was in Leicester for three months before joining the Lowestoft Secondary School at Worksop. The following, is an extract from Neville's own written account.

THE SCHOOL CAME SUCCESSFULLY THROUGH

Neville in the garden at Naseby Road, Leicester 1940 with an Anderson shelter in the background

In 1940, my brother Barry and I attended Church Road Junior School in Lowestoft. In the uncertain situation of the time, my parents decided they would prefer to arrange a private evacuation for Barry and me. Thus, Barry and I went to live with Jack and Irene Ball, at 29 Naseby Road, Leicester. Barry and I would play in the large rear garden there, where there was an Anderson air-raid shelter. I had taken the scholarship examination in Lowestoft, and having passed, I went to Worksop in August 1940, to join Lowestoft Secondary School which was sharing the premises of the local Central School.

Barry remained in Leicester for three more years and eventually joined the Secondary School, in Worksop, in September 1943. However, in September 1940, he moved down Naseby Road, to live with the family of Mr and Mrs Fred Smitten. Tragically, Jack and Irene Ball were killed, together with Mr and Mrs Pulford, at 59 Ireton Road, when the house was struck by an H E bomb (High Explosive), on 14th September 1940. I was not told of this until much later. The Smittens remained family friends long after the War, and spent several holidays with us, in Lowestoft. Years later, when I was an undergraduate at Nottingham University, I visited them several times.

On arrival in Worksop, I found that I would be sharing a billet with my best friend, Alan Howling, at the home of Mr and Mrs Brookfield. From the beginning, we were treated as members of the family. Sensibly, we were expected to do a small share of the household chores – I particularly remember, my introduction to my first electric vacuum cleaner. The school shared the premises of Worksop Central School, working mornings and afternoons on alternate weeks. Much time was spent, in the nearby Carnegie Public Library and we became avid readers.

As Christmas approached, it was felt that pupils, staff, and foster parents, all deserved a break and arrangements were made for us to get to Lowestoft, for the school holidays. Rail travel, in wartime, was often very slow, as priority was given to military and freight traffic. However, we were given a special coach and hitched on to passenger trains for various sections of the journey. Barry stayed in Leicester for Christmas and my mother and I joined him there for a few days before I returned to Worksop.

Towards the end of the second term, we had to leave the Brookfields, our foster parents, unexpectedly and we had a very short stay with Mr and Mrs Nutter, who lived nearby. In about May 1941, we moved to our new billet with a youngish couple, Sydney and Ethel Fletcher. Mr Fletcher was a plumber by trade and both he and his wife were deeply involved in the Scouting movement. Sydney Fletcher died in 1987 but Alan and I had the opportunity to meet up again with Mrs Fletcher and her son, Tony, during the Reunion day trip to Worksop in 1990. I carried on a correspondence with Ethel Fletcher until her death in 2003.

Most of the pupils in the school returned to Lowestoft for the long summer holiday of 1941. My parents decided Barry and I should not stay in the town and they arranged for us, and my mother, to lodge in Earsham, near Bungay. Dad was a full-time fire-fighter, in the National Fire Service, during the war and part-time beyond.

Back in Worksop, we began some new subjects: Latin, Chemistry, and Physics. There were no proper laboratory facilities in the central School but the Technical College in Blyth Road was well equipped. With this additional accommodation, we were able to work almost a full school day.

At the end of 1941 we had another change of billet when the Fletchers were no longer able to look after us. We moved to the home of Darwin and Margaret Bartrop, where we stayed for the next two years. Across the road, at no 29, was Miss Winifred Boothroyd and she invited us to play bagatelle, or look at her stamp collection. Her brother Basil Boothroyd, was an author of humorous books and articles and later became an assistant editor of Punch magazine.

At school, I enjoyed classes, especially the laboratory work in physics and chemistry and mathematics. An innovative feature of our curriculum, was a Saturday morning programme of activities. There were no formal classes but they sometimes ended with an informal concert. I can still remember some of the verses of what became the School Song and sung to the tune of Solomon Levi, which usually closed the proceedings. The chorus ran:

> 'We've come to Worksop, Worksop tra la la la
> All still in Worksop, Worksop tra la la la
> They mash the tea and wash the pots when we come home from school
> They say we're mardy when we cry, and mucky as a rule.'

Soon after we returned to Worksop from Lowestoft in October 1943, the older classes had the opportunity to work on local farms, which were desperately short of labour, to bring in the harvest. During the first week we worked on potato-picking and some beet-pulling, and then we had a few days of similar work on another farm. We were paid 8d per hour, plus a small bonus and altogether we each earned over £2, which was to us a substantial sum.

In December 1943 Alan and I left the Bartrops and stayed, for a few weeks with a young couple, with a son aged about two years. They had only recently moved into the house, which was still not fully furnished. I remember the bedroom, which Alan and I shared, contained little apart from two camp beds. They were kind people and did their best to look after us.

In April 1944 we moved to our final billet in Worksop with an elderly couple. He was a retired coal-miner and a man of few words. We were their first evacuees and although they were a pleasant couple and made us comfortable, they regarded us more as lodgers than members of the family. By then, we were old enough and independent enough, to cope with this and it worked quite well.

After the intensive bombing of Lowestoft in 1941 and early 1942 the number of air raids began to tail off in 1943 and by early 1944, pressure began to mount for the school to return to Lowestoft.

We had been nearly four years in Worksop and although local people had been most hospitable in accepting us into their homes, there was a feeling that we were beginning to outstay our welcome. In February 1944 six sixth-form boys wrote to the Lowestoft Journal urging our return in somewhat immoderate terms. The headmaster, Mr Brooks, naturally felt that the boys had gone behind his back and should have discussed the matter with him first and he took appropriate disciplinary action. However, the sentiments expressed by the boys were echoed by many parents and my father wrote a supporting letter to the Journal. The matter rested there for several months but discussions must have gone on behind the scenes because, in July 1944, we were suddenly informed that the school would be returning to Lowestoft the following week, taking all its equipment with it. Reserved coaches were laid on for our return journey by train. My last memory of Worksop is of trudging through the darkened streets to the railway station with my friend Alan, accompanied by our 'foster-father' wheeling our hand luggage on the frame of his bicycle.

Ironically, our return to Lowestoft coincided with the start of the German V-1 Flying Bomb 'Doodlebug' campaign. These unmanned missiles were mainly targeted at London and those which passed over Lowestoft were launched from points off the east coast, by converted Heinkel HE 111 bombers, based in north Germany. The doodlebugs raised concern with the local education authority and in August 1944 a letter was sent to the parents of every pupil asking them to vote whether or not, the school should go back to Worksop. The Mayor, Major S W Humphreys, who was also chairman of the Borough Higher Education Committee, received criticism in the local press for this action, implying that the Committee was shirking its responsibility and should have made the decision themselves. Major Humphreys replied vigorously in a long letter in the Journal and in the event we stayed in Lowestoft and the task began of getting the school buildings back in some sort of shape for re-opening. In retrospect, I am full of admiration for the school staff, who must have worked very hard during the summer holidays to do this, whilst at the same time having to get their own homes sorted out, after four years absence.

We pupils were blissfully unaware of all this and thoroughly enjoyed our summer break. The School duly re-opened in the autumn and quickly settled into a routine. Looking back I realise that money must have been very tight but we were used to war-time austerity and 'making do'. Pupil numbers increased sharply and the staffing situation was critical, especially on the science side, as two long-serving masters had retired and other former masters were still serving in the Armed Forces. Nevertheless the school had come successfully through a very difficult period, had managed to retain its identity, and was ready to move forward. It was good to be back in Lowestoft.

After the war I attended Nottingham University and eventually I became a professor of physics. This led to a career of teaching physics in universities around the world and in particular in Africa.

Lowestoft Secondary School 1942 Form 2a, in Worksop.
Neville on the middle row second from the right.

MAPS OF LOWESTOFT SCHOOLS

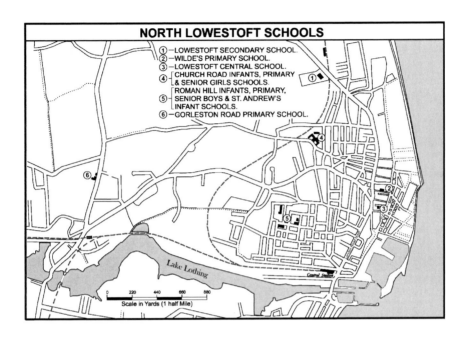

NORTH LOWESTOFT SCHOOLS

1 —LOWESTOFT SECONDARY SCHOOL.
2 —WILDE'S PRIMARY SCHOOL.
3 —LOWESTOFT CENTRAL SCHOOL.
4 —CHURCH ROAD INFANTS, PRIMARY & SENIOR GIRLS SCHOOLS.
5 —ROMAN HILL INFANTS, PRIMARY, SENIOR BOYS & ST. ANDREW'S INFANT SCHOOLS.
6 —GORLESTON ROAD PRIMARY SCHOOL.

Lake Lothing

Central Station

0   220   440   660   880
Scale in Yards (1 half Mile)

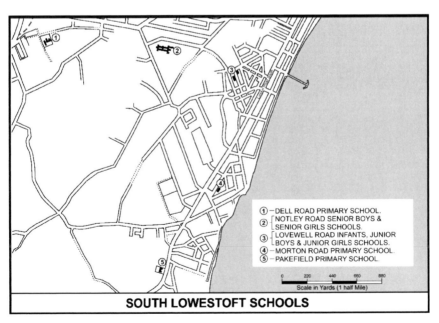

1 —DELL ROAD PRIMARY SCHOOL.
2 —NOTLEY ROAD SENIOR BOYS & SENIOR GIRLS SCHOOLS.
3 —LOVEWELL ROAD INFANTS, JUNIOR BOYS & JUNIOR GIRLS SCHOOLS.
4 —MORTON ROAD PRIMARY SCHOOL.
5 —PAKEFIELD PRIMARY SCHOOL.

0   220   440   660   880
Scale in Yards (1 half Mile)

SOUTH LOWESTOFT SCHOOLS

EVACUATION TO DERBYSHIRE/NOTTINGHAMSHIRE

A. Lead up to Evacuation

Once the German army had occupied the Low Countries (Belgium and Holland) in May 1940 the threat of invasion increased and it was thought the most likely route for this to take place was the short route across the Channel to any one of the East Coast ports. As a result, in late May 1940, plans were drawn up by the UK government to evacuate close to 50,000 children, aged between 5 and 15 years, from 18 coastal towns in the south east.

Lowestoft was one of these towns where the order was given to close all the schools and consequently the children from these schools were evacuated in June 1940 by trains to towns/villages in Derbyshire and Nottinghamshire.

Fortunately, teachers and helpers were allowed to travel with the children, other than those called up to serve in the forces. Parents were not allowed to even say goodbye to their children at the station to avoid congestion. Minimum age for evacuation was 5 years old, exceptions to this being when there was an older child to travel with a younger sibling of 3-4 years of age.

Pupils Evacuated from Lowestoft Schools

School	Number of Pupils Evacuated
Roman Hill	615
Church Road	593
Lovell Road	360
Secondary	349
Notley Road	277
Central *	139
Oulton Broad	138
Wildes *	107

Dell Road	93
Morton Road	92
Pakefield	56
St. Andrews	23
Total	**2842**

Source: Extracts from the Chronicles of Lowestoft Schools, Register in Evacuation.

N.B. Teachers and helpers account for approximately 10% of this figure.
* Badly damaged by bombing.

B. The Rail Journey from Lowestoft to Derbyshire

Therefore, on Sunday 2nd June 1940, around 3,000 children left Lowestoft in five trains heading to Derbyshire and Nottinghamshire. These children were facing a long journey, approximately 6 hours in length, without their parents. For some it was the first time they had been on a train.

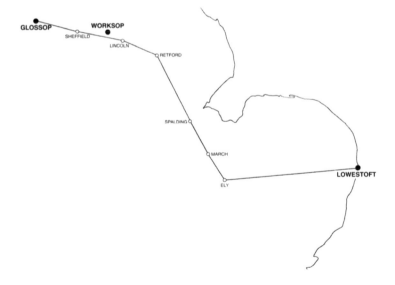

N.B. Lowestoft to Glossop approximately 200 miles.

The children were only allowed to take a minimum of luggage, literally what they could carry. The individual items were listed in a handwritten letter about the train journey by a Lowestoft teacher, Miss Hogg:

gas masks, identity cards, ration cards, food for the day, a change of underclothing, hankies, plimsoles, tooth brush, comb, etc.

In addition to teachers travelling with the evacuees, a wide range of adults were involved at each end and on the journey as shown below:

- Mothers travelling with babies
- Liaison officers
- Nurses
- WVS
- Salvation Army
- Billeting Officers

So what were the evacuees memories of that day? All remember it was very hot and when the train stopped at stations they were handed water by the station staff and local people.

However, the evacuees could not recall the names of the stations they passed through as all the nameplates had been taken down to confuse the enemy if they landed.

To show how serious the situation was, one evacuee remembers the trains were escorted by a number of Spitfires and Hurricanes. For some, there was excitement about what was happening, however the children did not realise the imminent danger they were escaping from.

Those heading to Glossop, remember vividly the train travelling through a long tunnel and this in fact was the 'famous' Woodhead Tunnel, some 3 miles long, passing under the Pennines between Sheffield and Manchester. In those days, the carriages did not have much lighting so for a few minutes, the children were virtually plunged into darkness which must have been terrifying, particularly for the very young children, already traumatised by the journey away from home.

C. Arrival at Host Towns and Villages

On arrival, the children where possible were kept in their school groups and taken to a number of designated host towns/villages. These ranged from a small cluster of villages in east Derbyshire with less than 10,000 population to two fairly large towns, Worksop and Glossop.

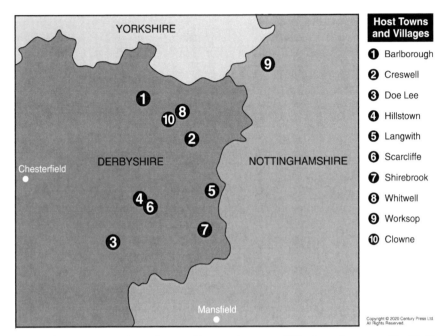

N.B. Glossop approximately 40 miles north west of Worksop between Sheffield and Manchester Worksop to Creswell approximately 10 miles.

The teachers played a very important part in this whole evacuation exercise to first look after and calm the children on the train, then to make sure that they were settled in suitable billets.

The memory for most of the children was that after their long and tiring journey on the train, they were then taken by bus or coach to a central place within their host village, such as the village hall, church or cinema.

The local people would then come and select which evacuee(s) was most suitable for them – this may have been acceptable for some but not good for the ones that were among the last to be picked out.

Once settled, the evacuees were encouraged to write a postcard home to let their parents know where they were staying.

In virtually all of the towns/villages, there was not enough room at the schools to cope with the influx of the evacuees. Eventually the procedure adopted in most cases was a shift system dividing the day in half, whereby local children attended school in the morning and the evacuees in the afternoon and this procedure was then reversed each week. The local boys saw this as a plus point for putting up with the evacuees as they had less time at school.

It was not possible in all cases to keep siblings and close school friends together. Some evacuees stayed just a few months, became homesick and went home. Others reached an age where they went out to work, and in those days the school leaving age was as young as 14 years old. A few of these eventually settled permanently in the area and went on to marry local people.

Prior to the arrival of the evacuees, local billeting officers had been round to each household to ascertain what empty accommodation was available. It was in fact compulsory for households to take in evacuees if they had available bed space. Some were reluctant to do this, but failure to comply could result in a fine. Others, without children, welcomed the chance to have an evacuee staying in their home. In fact, in some of these cases, this led to the foster parents wanting to adopt the evacuee and then at the end of the war it would become a tug of war between the biological parents and the foster parents as to where the child should finish up.

The evacuation on this scale can now be seen as a massive logistical exercise, a virtual nightmare, arranging for 3,000 pupils from 12 schools to be billeted at just as many towns and villages across two counties.

D. Stories Recorded

In all, 40 evacuee stories are featured in the book, mostly relating to evacuees who left from Lowestoft. The majority of these stories were obtained by way of an interview by the authors using a voice recorder. The remainder were either written by the evacuees themselves or by a close relative or friend.

The distribution of the Lowestoft evacuee stories according to the host towns/villages they stayed at is shown in following table.

Number of Lowestoft evacuee stories

Town or Village	Number of Stories
Glossop	9
Creswell	7
Whitwell	5
Barlborough	2
Hillstown	2
Langwith	2
Shirebrook	2
Doe Lee	1
Scarcliffe	1
Worksop	1

For this book it was decided to profile two of the towns/villages, namely Glossop and Creswell, which incidentally had the most stories. However they were quite different with regard to population, industrial activities and geographical position.

There were major differences between Lowestoft and reception areas.

TOWN SIZE	Mainly large to small
INDUSTRY	Fishing to mining and textile industries
LOCATION	Coastal to inland, no sea
HOUSING	Small to large and vice versa
SPEECH	Very different accents, sounded foreign!
EDUCATION	Local children in morning evacuees in afternoon, reversed each week
FACILITIES	Outside toilets, no running water
FAMILY STRUCTURE	Some had no children and wanted to adopt the evacuee
POST WAR	Some stayed, found jobs and got married

One of the major objectives was to establish how the host towns/villages felt about the arrival of the evacuees and a further insight was gained from the three stories obtained from the host village end.

E. Creswell (Host Village)

Stories included in the book from Creswell evacuees:
Melville Canham, Clive Capps, Peter Chenery, Margaret Day, Iris Day, Trudy James, Kathleen Wilton

This village is not to be confused with Cresswell, 4 miles north of Ashington in Northumberland, and was a reason for changing the spelling of this Derbyshire village to Creswell. This is a small village with a population of around 5,000 about 10 miles from the larger town of Worksop. At the time of the evacuation the whole village was centred around the coal mine there, in terms of jobs and accommodation provided for the miners.

Unfortunately after the war, the coal mine was closed in 1950 following a very serious accident when 80 miners died. Creswell is also well-known for its unique archaeological site, the Crags (previously spelt Craggs). This is an intricate formation of very old caves and rocky terrain.

Around 300 evacuees arrived in Creswell from three Lowestoft schools, namely Roman Hill, St. Andrews and Dell Road. This resulted in a considerable impact on the local people which was particularly noticeable at the schools where the number of children attending was virtually doubled.

After the train arrived, the evacuees were taken to the local Regors cinema, where the future foster parents assembled to select the most suitable children, in their minds, for their homes.

It was fortunate that one of the local children, Enid Hibbert, is still living there and her story mentions the arrival of the evacuee children and her parents went on to take in an evacuee, Iris Day, who became a lifelong friend of Enid.

In later years, Enid was very much involved in helping to organise reunions at the Creswell end when evacuees from Lowestoft came by coach to Creswell and they and the local people were able to meet.

Visit to Creswell by Lowestoft evacuees, July 2007.
Source: Clive Capps

Creswell also now has a history society which takes a keen interest in the evacuee story. So the link between the two ends is as strong as ever.

F. Glossop (Host Village)

Stories included in book from Glossop evacuees:
Ivan Barber, Keith Bellward, Margery Chilvers, John Clarke, Margaret Ellis, Bryan Howard, Alma Mingay, Gordon Sewell, Neville Skinner.

A total of around 500 evacuees arrived in Glossop. In contrast to Creswell this town had a much larger population of over 30,000.

Compared with Creswell this town, at the time of the evacuation, was predominantly a market town, known best for its weaving industry. It is midway between two major cities, Manchester and Sheffield and some evacuees recall seeing the sky light up with flames from the bombing of these cities.

Here an interesting story written by a local resident Neil Williams who has a connection with the family of an evacuee. It describes the thinking behind the establishment of a link between the railway stations at Lowestoft (departure) and Glossop (arrival).

In 2010, LEA arranged for a plaque to be placed at Lowestoft Railway Station to mark the departure of the evacuees on 2nd June 1940. Then in 2017, the Friends of Glossop Station inspired by member Neil Williams placed a plaque at Glossop Railway Station to mark the arrival of the evacuees.

Returning Home

Unexpectedly, it emerged from the stories that many of the evacuee children were not happy about returning home particularly those who had stayed away as long as five years. There were many reasons for this, some of which are shown below:

- Home had changed
- More siblings had arrived in the family
- Parents had moved house
- Friends had moved on elsewhere
- Schools had been bombed
- Return to a town virtually flattened by bombing
- Parents, relations and friends had been lost or injured
- Felt guilty about leaving parents to face bombing
- Missed foster parents

Revisiting the Host Villages

The link between Lowestoft and the host towns/villages was further rekindled by the LEA deciding in 2006 to organise coach trips to the Derbyshire area once a year. As a result, each year a coach full of evacuees would arrive in Derbyshire and groups of evacuees would be dropped off at the villages they had previously stayed at. This enabled the evacuees in some cases to revisit their foster homes and in a number of instances meet the children, now adults, who were living there at the time.

A GLOSSOP LOWESTOFT CONNECTION
Neil Williams' Story, May 2020

My story begins in North, Wales where I was born in the 1950s and lived with my family for my early years. Then, due to my father's change of job, we moved to Glossop. It has been my home since then apart from a four year further education period in Nottingham. Here I trained to be a secondary school teacher. In Glossop I attended St. Luke's Junior School and on my mile and a half walk to school I called each day en route to walk with Alan* (name changed) whose father had been a Lowestoft evacuee. He had remained in Glossop at the end of the war and married a local lady. Alan was their only child. Every holiday the family travelled to Lowestoft to meet with relatives and the evacuation story behind these frequent visits was explained to me. So I grew up always knowing the story. In later years I used to see occasional references to it in the local press. David Jones the long standing Editor of The Glossop Chronicle had once worked with Peter Glover (married to the late Sheila an evacuee). David has therefore always shown a keen interest in the evacuation and has published many a story over the years. I have also known Sheila Webster, widow of Ian, for a number of years too. Sheila has given many talks locally to organisations about the evacuation a key component being Ian's small leather suitcase that he brought to Glossop!

Fast forward now to 2016. I was on holiday in Norwich and took a day trip by train to Lowestoft a place that I had not visited for thirty years. As Chairman of a local voluntary group - Friends of Glossop Station - I always take a keen interest in stations and I look to see how they are being cared for. We have over a number of years, as a group, enhanced the appearance of Glossop station with gardens, floral displays art work, and poetry. We regularly hold community events at the station often involving children. To my surprise one of the first things I spotted inside the booking hall at Lowestoft station was an attractive commemorative plaque marking the departure on June 2nd 1940 of several hundred child evacuees to five Derbyshire and Nottinghamshire towns. Glossop was one of these! It struck me forcibly that nothing existed in Glossop to mark their arrival. And that there was a real danger that the story of the evacuation could be lost especially for future generations. An idea was then born! Back in Glossop at our next Friends of Glossop Station group meeting I sought support to create a commemorative plaque marking the evacuees' arrival at the station. There was enthusiastic and wholehearted commitment to create a plaque along with a commemorative event. During autumn 2016 and winter 2017 plans started to take shape. With Sheila's help we made contact with Chris Brookes Secretary of Lowestoft Evacuation Committee. Chris backed our plans and provided us with invaluable help and resources. We also learned that Chris had been running annual trips with former Lowestoft evacuees every summer to Glossop. A date of significance, June 2nd 2017, was chosen to unveil the plaque at the station with guests from Lowestoft and Glossop.

During the winter Penny Greenwood, a FOGS' member, and myself visited with invitation the homes of evacuees who chose to remain in Glossop after the end of the war. We were often moved by stories of fortitude and stoicism. And good humour! In addition Chris lent me a book he had written "When Will I See You Again?" which widened my knowledge and understanding. I was particularly moved by a two verse poem written by Kathleen Barber recounting her feelings returning to Glossop after a fifty year gap. The last lines of both verses read, "Thank God for a town that cared" a moving tribute to the people of Glossop. In February 2017 we received permission from Northern, our local rail company, to hold the event at the station. We received funding towards the cost of the plaque from the High Peak and Hope Valley Community Rail Partnership. Fortunately one of our own members, Simon Denvers, was able to create and produce the plaque. In Lowestoft we received help from Martin Halliday Community Rail Officer for the Lowestoft, Ipswich, and Great Yarmouth railway lines in publicising our plans. To add realism to the event we decided to dress four local children as evacuees and have them arrive by train on the day of the event. Their arrival provided a poignant highlight of the day. Witnessing these children standing next to the real adult evacuees on the platform brought a lump to many a throat.

On June 2nd 2017 over eighty people joined us at the station many more than we had expected. Local dignitaries and railway managers were in attendance too but all the attention was deservedly on our special evacuee guests from Lowestoft. What memories these scenes must have evoked in their minds on this 77th anniversary of the arrival at Glossop station. Chris Brookes and myself led the welcome speeches.

This was followed by the reading of Kathleen Barber's poem. Alma Mingay and Bryan Howard then duly unveiled the plaque and remained in position for many photos! Our local station café TWIG provided refreshments along with home-made biscuits for all guests distributed by our evacuee children. All our guests received a specially designed souvenir memento card of the day which included Kathleen's poem.

Since that memorable day further reunion events have taken place in Glossop and Lowestoft in 2018 and 2019. I have been able to join in the summer events at Lowestoft and have enjoyed these very much. Such has been the rekindling of interest in the evacuee story that we commissioned a special information board to go on display in the Waiting Room at Glossop station telling the story with pictures. (This information can be viewed online on a special Lowestoft section on Friends of Glossop station website.) Paul Marsh who created and designed the board made an exact replica which he kindly donated to Lowestoft. With Martin Halliday's help Greater Anglia Trains agreed to the installation of this board in the booking hall of Lowestoft station in 2018.

I took the board to Lowestoft by train and on its formal presentation and launch later in the summer I told the evacuees that the board had experienced the railway journey that they had made but in reverse!

Of the many community events that I have been involved with at Glossop station over the years the Lowestoft reunions and commemorations stand out. I feel a sense of pride that this important story is once again recognized and respected. But my contribution is but one little piece of the jigsaw that makes up the story of the evacuation. So in recognition of the collective care given by the people of Glossop to the evacuee children of Lowestoft I would like to conclude with the moving words from Kathleen Barber's poem.

Neil Williams May 2020

Kathleen Barber of Park Road, Lowestoft was aged 7 when she came with her 6 year old brother and other pupils from Lovewell Road Girls' School to Glossop. Her poem sums up her feelings when she returned to her childhood refuge.

The woman viewed the market place
Its stalls still standing bare;
A silent witness to a day
That she remembered there.
When children stood around the place,
Or sat down on a stall.
Then people came and picked them out,
She clearly could recall.
For some a boy, for some a girl,
For some just one of each.
Her memory spanned so many years
That day's events to reach.
Some had wept, all were scared.
Thank God that town held folk who cared.

The woman viewed the market place
Its stalls still standing bare;
A silent witness in that town
To all that happened there.
When as a child she stood,
Or sat down on a stall.
A little case clutched to her side,
She clearly could recall.
The gas mask in a cardboard box,
Its strap slung on her shoulder.
But that was fifty years ago,
Was she really that much older?
An evacuee, she'd been so scared.
Thank God for a billet with folk who cared.

Link between two railway stations – Lowestoft and Glossop

Lowestoft Rail Station Plaque

Lowestoft 2010 – Local Mayor and LEA Chairman Brian Baxter
with the plaque to be placed at Lowestoft station
Source: Chris Brooks

Glossop Railway Station Plaque

Glossop 2017 – Unveiling of plaque at Glossop railway station by
evacuees Alma Mingay and Bryan Howard
Source: John Kimpton

Enid Hibbert was a local girl aged six living in Creswell when the Lowestoft evacuees arrived in June 1940. Her mother, Mrs Cottrell, took in Iris Day (née Wilton), one of the Lowestoft evacuees aged seven. This is an extract from Enid's own written account.

LIKE A SISTER

Enid

I was still at Infant School when war was declared in September 1939. The first change to children's lives in Creswell was the securing of a place of safety for them in case of a daylight air raid while they were at school. Those living nearby went home when the air raid siren sounded but as I lived at the far end of the village, I was sent to a shop across the road from the school where people whose surname was Glossop looked after me. Then came the issuing of gas marks, horrible rubber contraptions which we had to practise wearing. I remember the lessons on doing this. The rule was they had to be carried everywhere in a cardboard box.

As well as school, I also attended the Primitive Methodist Chapel on Sundays. It was on one of these Sundays, June 2nd 1940, when coming out of chapel, I could see crowds of children gathered on the steps of the local Regors Cinema which was across the road. That memory will remain forever in my mind. It is interesting to note the background to that building. It was built by the Rogers family in 1939 to replace the Electric Palace which burnt down the year before. The cinema was given that name as the name Regors is basically Rogers spelt backwards. (Mr J. A. Rogers was the owner and managing director for many years.)

I had no idea what was happening but on reaching my home, 21 Model Village, there were two girls, about my age, standing there. One was named Muriel and the other was Iris Wilton. Muriel was to live with us whilst Iris was initially billeted with my Grandparents across the road at 28 Model Village. How bewildering it must have been for these evacuees, to come from a coastal fishing town to a coal mining village. No one realised the trauma which manifested itself in this situation. I have not read anything which says help was given to children with this huge disturbance in their lives or to those in the receiving families. It was a case of get on with it. Parents must have been distraught at sending their children at a very young age into the unknown.

For me, it was a complete change from being an only child to being eventually one of three. Iris lived with my grandparents for a while but spent time with us before eventually coming to live with us. Muriel found it very difficult to settle and who can blame her, being uprooted to another way of life and family? Soon my mother realised that the best thing for her was to return to Lowestoft. This she did. Iris crossed the road to our house and then stayed five years and virtually became my foster sister as we were less than a year apart in age.

Soon after the evacuees came there was a very bad air raid on Sheffield, just 20 miles away, when the Germans bombed the city for several nights. The sky was lit up with a red glow as the bombs fell. Earlier, shelters had been built for such an event. One had been built in the park almost opposite our house. We ran in the dark towards its safety. This was the only time I can remember using them. When we heard the siren go at the pit we rushed downstairs and sheltered in a small place under the stairs where we three girls slept on a mattress. We learned to distinguish the sound of German planes and were so relieved when their sound faded into the distance. We were safe for another day.

Children in Creswell began to share their school premises with Lowestoft children – one week we had morning lessons there and the next we went in the afternoons only. People opened their 'front rooms' for classes and many nature walks including rosehip picking afternoons took place. Somehow our education didn't seem to suffer. Home life went on – not much change for the Creswell children really.

Throughout this time Iris and I played as children do. Usually a crowd of children would gather on the street to play together. Double summertime helped as it would be light for longer. Iris' sister Sheila was living with the Fretwell family on Bakers Street in Creswell but very often came to see Iris and came to our birthday parties. The local cinema had Saturday morning matinees so we would go there too. My Mum and Dad were great ballroom dancers and my Dad played drums in a band. So we would go to dances with them and dance together. We always went to dances on Boxing Day evening and New Year's Eve. Iris' mother and, I think, her father came to see their children and I think they would have stayed with us. I remember seeing Iris' older sister Violet who was billeted in Langwith and also her brother Eric. I don't know where he was but I know my mother was very worried about where he was living. She wrote to Mrs Wilton and before long Mr Wilton, who was in the army, came to fetch him back home.

Throughout the time Iris was with us I think I can safely say that she was treated the same as I was. My mother sewed clothes for us – if I had a new dress so did Iris. I hope there was no distinction at all. At meal times we would play spelling and number games, all light heartedly, as my parents wanted both of us to do well at school. We both passed the scholarship plus to enable us to go to Grammar School.

This meant Iris would have to go back to Lowestoft to continue her education. Both my parents thought the world of Iris and would have loved her to stay but of course her parents wanted her back.

Iris grew up and married Ralph Day who was also evacuated to Creswell. For many years Iris and Ralph often stayed with my Mum and Dad and at times with me and my husband Barrie. Iris never lost touch. The last time Iris saw my mother was when she came to stay with me and we had a family party to celebrate my Mother's 90th birthday. Iris was and is part of my family and of course she knew everyone there. Sadly my mother died 2 years later but Iris couldn't make the journey up here. However she wrote a poem about my parents which the vicar read at the funeral service (it was too moving for me to try and read).

At a reunion in Creswell prior to the 2008 one, we met Clive Capps, secretary of the Lowestoft Evacuee Reunion Association. We helped him find his billet which was a farm house close to the Crags where at the time a young boy named John Boffey lived with his parents. Clive was keen to track down John and the breakthrough in the search, nearly 70 years later, was that my husband Barrie went to school with John Boffey. Fortunately, Barrie did remember where he went to university and also that he took a job in Cardiff. Clive followed up that lead and eventually located where he was living in Cardiff and shortly after met with him and his wife Karen in central Cardiff – what an incredible reunion of 2 young boys after nearly 70 years!

I have always been interested in local history, particularly of our two adjacent villages, Creswell and Elmton. I joined the local history group and became secretary, a post I still hold to this day.

I played a major part in putting together a number of books written on the history of the immediate area, the schools, and one specifically covering the WW1 and WW2 years. In addition, as secretary, I find speakers to provide talks at our meetings.

Since then Iris has been back with the evacuees several times and she and her friend Jean stayed with us when we had a big reunion in Creswell in July 2008. Barrie and I went to Lowestoft for their 70th evacuees' reunion in 2010 and also had a holiday nearby when Iris' sister-in-law Margaret and her son Peter, now sadly gone, showed us some of the interesting places around. I still write to Iris and also Margaret so the link with Lowestoft continues after nearly 80 years.

A Small Tribute in the Life of Dorothy May Cottrell

Dorothy and Fred
Took into their loving home,
A small evacuee.
Homesick, forlorn,
For her to share.
Cared for and loved
As much as Enid, their own.
In sickness and health
Not much wealth,
Scraped knees and bruises.
Faults forgiven,
Praised, hair done up in rags for
Sunday School Anniversary.
Bursting with pride
To say correct lines,

As two girls sat shyly
Side by side
In dresses made with loving care
By the true Star of the show
Dorothy May, stitching Taffeta
Of pink and green, green and pink,
So many hours put lovingly in.

Dorothy May,
Is it the murmur of the trees,
Gently swaying in the wind,
Or is it Dorothy May and Fred
Now united, having their last waltz?

Iris Day (nee Wilton)
November 1st 2001

Enid on the left with evacuee Iris Day on the right.
Enid's mother, May, is at the back.

Arnold 'Bill' Legood, the youngest of five children, was 12 years old when he was evacuated from a school in Lowestoft to Whitwell, Derbyshire in June 1940. He became a lifelong friend of Tom Wood, the little boy aged 4 whose home was the billet he stayed at.

Sadly, Arnold passed away in 2015 and so this story was written by Tom Wood.

THE NEW ARRIVAL

Arnold L. and Tom W. 1940

Whitwell, Derbyshire billet

"Please call me Bill," were the first words that Arnold Legood spoke to me on the day that heralded the arrival of the evacuees into Whitwell, mostly from the Lowestoft area but including some from London and Kent. With all their worldly possessions clutched to their chest, a gas mask in a cardboard box over their shoulder and a brown label attached to the collar of their coat, a more pitiful assembly of frightened, disorientated youngsters would have been hard to imagine.

Arnold was the only one of the five children to be evacuated as the three above him in age were all too old to be evacuated and Reginald, his younger brother, was too young to be evacuated.

Our family along with others had been asked to give temporary homes to those so affected and my father, Tom Wood Senior, my mother Dora and myself Tom Junior, were there to welcome them into our homes without question. The method of allocating the youngsters to their new respective homes was never known to me but one way or another, each and every one was in their new home by nightfall. It seemed that initially there were too many according to the numbers previously suggested and it was soon evident that not all of the evacuees had been found a home. Father was asked if he could manage another. After a word with mother he said yes, and Arnold and John, from London, joined us. As the first few weeks passed and a state of give and take was established, it would have been hard to find two lads so different in character and mannerisms and it soon became apparent that John was going to be more than a handful. Whereas Arnold was eager to fit in, John was unsociable, defiant and destructive and continually talked of his "patch" in Bermondsey. Somewhere in my diaries I have his full name but it's not one that I care to remember and after three months he was removed from our care and we were told he had gone back to the London area after two weeks with another family.

Arnold settled in well after insisting that he hated the name Arnold, and would we call him Bill. We tried this without success as my Grandfather was called Bill and my second name was William, shortened to "Bill". Sometimes this caused mayhem but eventually Arnold accepted it as it was, why he wanted to be called Bill not even his family ever knew. Although we were hard pushed to make ends meet father had a sparetime second job which helped to put icing on the cake and there was always something to give at birthdays and Christmas. When mother did the shopping, the grocer would always wrap a little extra over and above what the ration book allowed, saying, "there's a bit extra for the evacuee".

The influx of hundreds of these displaced youngsters created a huge social problem and many local youngsters who were ready to start school for the first time suddenly found themselves delayed for a year. Normal classes were split into two and they would attend either morning or afternoon on a rotating basis. Local chapels and community centres were converted into temporary classrooms and teachers found from those who were considered "proficient to teach". I don't recall ever finding a teacher or pupil who didn't benefit from this sympathetic approach and it was a credit to the youngsters that they responded with dignity after all they had been through.

Feeding the extra numbers was not a problem in a farming village as most householders with enough garden usually kept a pig or two and very often the government official, whose job it was to purchase all private meat stocks for the Armed Forces, would somehow miscount the numbers. This accidental error was usually rewarded with a crate of sausages, ham and pork pies, collected at night, a couple of days before Christmas or delivered to a pre-arranged destination.

Clothing them was another matter and the weird and wonderful ways of keeping a shirt on a back was unbelievable. Trousers with frayed turn ups would be cut off at the knees, the waist would be reduced by cutting a vee out of the back and sewing the waist back up. Skirts for the girls were cunningly crafted from adult ones, shortened, then cut into a number of sections from the waist to the hem and placed in the linen basket. They were then picked at random from the basket and sewn back together to form a shortened multi coloured, patterned skirt and it was possible for a good seamstress to get as many as five smaller skirts from two adult ones. Dipped in a dye they were very presentable. Many of the evacuees learned skills and crafts from the villages which they would never have learned had it not been for the war and whilst this did not compensate them for their loss, it was a way of bringing them closer to the family.

As family members they would be invited to the various parties and functions that were the hub of the village. Not only did they meet up with others who came with them and whom they had not known before but some very close friendships were started with the locals which lasted for many years afterwards including marriages. After a year or so all the doubts as to how they would react were forgotten and some of them were beginning to prove an asset to the community. Arnold was becoming the big brother I didn't have and proving to be a great help to father when it came to looking after the greyhounds, pigeons and allotment. As the days passed into weeks, the initial feeling of "us and them" coined by those who did not participate, turned into one of acceptance and the youngsters gradually melted into their respective new homes. As Arnold grew and made new friends, his visits to Mr Kirk the local butcher for horse meat for the greyhounds became less of a chore when friendships developed between himself and their evacuees, Gracie, Daisy and Ethel (also from Lowestoft) along with their own daughter Theo and another evacuee named Beryl Gooch who lived with the Baker family.

Of these four evacuees, only two returned home and this pattern was repeated many times elsewhere. Arnold being never one to push himself forward but always there to give a hand he became well liked and his above average height ensured that he had a reasonably calm passage at school. Mother encouraged him to write home at least two or three times a year but he always kept the letters short, the reason he said was because there would be nothing to talk about when he got back home after the war.

Those evacuees who did not know each other before arriving in Whitwell but from the same area gradually learned of each other's presence and whilst doing so would very often be seen in an isolated group at school. This apparently was to share any news which came in letters from home and was perfectly innocent, but others would often refer to the group as "The Escape Committee".

With the end of hostilities and the celebration parties came the tears and the farewells. Some did not want to return and stayed on, later to marry local youngsters and always to consider themselves "Whitwellians". Arnold returned home, settled back into his original family circle and spent his two years in "National Service" overseas. After demobilisation he was employed as a representative with a local brewery, later to become their service engineer when the firm was taken over. One of the other evacuees who returned home with Arnold was Beryl, the one who had lived with the Baker family throughout the same period and they were later married. Back home, Arnold had a younger brother named Reginald who on two occasions spent his holidays with us and was able to relate to the stories that Arnold had to tell. For some years Arnold and Beryl visited both us and those who had cared for her when it was needed. I am still in contact with Reginald and we plan to meet up later in the year.

POEMS

By Rose Chapman
Granddaughter of evacuee Clive Capps

EIGHTY YEARS AGO

Eighty years since we went away,

but our memories will always be here now to stay.

We were only just children when we travelled afar.

We are most proud for who we were and now are.

Evacuees are we and each has a story to share,

of our journeys from home and our experiences there.

So please not forget us now 80 years on,

even though time has passed and the war is now gone.

OUR JOURNEY

The Germans were coming! They would surely invade.

The outbreak of war meant that we couldn't have stayed.

The wireless boomed out into each house around an

evacuation area across the entire town.

Our parents were told that we could be protected

That they remain calm while we were collected

And taken in coaches to the main station

So we would be gone while the town suffered invasion.

There were hundreds of us, some aged only three

Who arrived with their siblings just like my brothers and me?

We were told we were off on the greatest adventure

But none of us knew until we would get there

'God bless you' there'd say but underneath I felt scared for

others were crying, but some did not care.

Others excited – the journey there would be fun

An experience that for many was our very first one.

All of us carried a change of clean clothes,

A hanky, a gas mask, a toothbrush, and comb.

My identity card and a ration book

All of these are the things I had took

As the train left the station, we gazed out – me and my brother

And saw a sea of faces and amongst them – our dear mother.

Crowds lined up the railings, frantically waving goodbye I

smiled and I waved and tried so hard not to cry.

When we finally arrived we were sent to a hall

All of us children – the big and the small.

I clung on to my brothers as hard as I could

While children were taken near the spot where we stood.

My new family came and they smiled with such joy to have
found their new son, a young little boy.
My brothers found homes with families elsewhere
And that's where we lived in the years we spent there.
We joined local schools and played in the street,
For some, future husbands and wives they did meet.
My experience with my family was a very happy one
for others it was tough and the struggle was long.
All of our memories are important beyond measure
For our experiences have shaped us and changed us forever.

MY GRANDAD

I look at my Grandad and just can't believe
The experiences he had and the things he has seen.
I'm so proud of my Grandad for going away.
I'm so intrigued and amazed by the things that he says
I wish I could have been there and seen it like he did.
How he went through such turmoil but still, he succeeded.
He was just a young boy at the age of only five
When his mother told him 'when you leave here, you'll be safe Clive'.
I teach small children of just five years old
So I can imagine how they felt when they had been told.
Split up from his brothers - that makes me so sad
But he talks of the good times with the new family he had.
Now 80 years on this book will make people aware
And give them some understanding, interest, and care
The Evacuees are precious and their stories too
Imagine how it would have felt if it had been you.

AFTERWORD

Meeting and recording the stories of the former evacuees, who gave their time so generously, has been an absolute pleasure and we hope we have done their stories credit.

It had been a very difficult decision for parents, who were encouraged by the government and the German bombs, to send their children away. 'The children are safer in the country' they were told. The Vera Lynn song 'Good Night Children Everywhere' asked the children to be brave.

The experiences of the child evacuees were diverse. Most children, but not all, received adequate treatment. However, all these children had to deal with displacement at a very young age. They bore home-sickness, separation from siblings, food rationing, and uncertainty about how long they would be away, for many it was years.

A great re-adjustment was needed when they arrived home with their lives being turned upside down again. In many cases, surprisingly, coming home was not a memorable or happy event as many things had changed. For some the ordeal was over, and for others another one began. For some opportunities had been lost and for others opportunities gained. Bonds with some parents were weakened and bonds with some foster parents were hard to break.

It was often difficult for host families who sometimes provided food and clothing from the family purse. However for some it was very rewarding.

World War Two ended in September 1945. However evacuation did not officially end until March 1946. The survival of these people, when children, has enabled them to be part of the greatly needed rebuilding of the town and the country.

We hope you enjoyed reading their stories.

MEET THE AUTHORS

SANDRA DELF (Author)

Sandra has always been interested in history. She is a volunteer at Lowestoft Museum and belongs to the Lowestoft U3A Family History Group. She has previously published 'Keep Smiling Through', Second World War - Letters from Prisoner of War Camps, a book consisting of letters written during WW2 by her father, a Lowestoft man, who was a prisoner of war in Italy and Germany.

Although a local person, Sandra has also lived in London and Australia. She has worked in various administrative roles and been employed by both The BBC and the Australian Broadcasting Commission.

Sandra became interested in the stories of local evacuees after meeting Clive Capps Vice-Chairman of the Lowestoft Evacuees Association and a former evacuee. With Clive's encouragement she is likely to remain connected to the Association.

CLIVE CAPPS (Evacuee Coordinator and Co-Author)

Clive was born in 1935 and was 5 years old when he was evacuated from Lowestoft to Derbyshire along with 3,000 other young children.

He obtained a BSc degree at Kings College London, married a Lowestoft girl Jean and spent most of his working life in Buckinghamshire. He held senior management posts in a number of industries. On retirement, he set up as an environmental consultant and became the co-editor of the magazine International Green Paper.

When he returned to Norfolk in the late 1990s he joined the Lowestoft Evacuee Association (LEA) and went on to become secretary in 2006. Then, in conjunction with the late Joan Shrubsall (a fellow evacuee), also formed a sub-group in Norwich.

In December 2018 Clive was appointed Vice-Chairman of the LEA and shortly after that, in conjunction with local author Sandra Delf, commenced work on an evacuee book of stories which would entail interviewing 40 evacuees to record their memories of events 80 years earlier. This book will commemorate the 80th Anniversary of the evacuees leaving Lowestoft.

Then finally in 2019 he visited the BEA headquarters to meet Karen Follows, general manager and James Roffey MBE, founder of BEA and formerly an evacuee.

BIBLIOGRAPHY

Boffey, James, *Send Them to Safety, a story of Great British Evacuation of the Second World War*. Published by Evacuee Reunion Association, 2009.

Brooks, Christopher J., *East Coast Evacuees*. Published by Christopher J. Brooks, 2001.

Brooks, Christopher J., *When Will I See You Again?* Published by Rushmere Publishing, 1991.

Brown, Mike, *A Child's War, Growing Up on the Home Front, 1939–1945*. Published by Sutton Publishing, 2000.

Collis, Bob and Baker, Simon, *The Air War Over Lowestoft 1939–1945*. Published by Lowestoft Aviation Society, 2011.

Inglis, Ruth, The Children's War. Evacuation 1939–1945. Published by William Collins, 1989.

Jackson, Dr Carlton, Who Will Take Our Children. Published by Methuen, London, 1985.

Longmate, Norman, *The Doodlebugs – The Story of the Flying Bombs, London*. Published by Hutchinson, 1981.

Mawson, Gillian, *Voices From The Past*. Published by Frontline Books, 2016.

Parsons, Martin L., *"I'll Take That One" Dispelling the Myths of Civil Evacuation*. Published by Beckett Karlson, 1998.

Government Evacuation Scheme Publications. Published by HMSO:
Notes for Billeting Officer and Voluntary Welfare Workers, 1941.
The Schools in Wartime, 1941.
Evacuation – Why & How? July 1939.

GLOSSARY

AFS – Auxiliary Fire Service.

Anderson Shelter – A small pre-made air raid shelter.

Armistice – A peace agreement.

ARP – Air Raid Precautions.

Barrage Balloons – A large balloon attached to the ground by metal cables that acts as an obstacle to low-flying enemy aircraft.

BEA – The British Evacuees Association.

Billeting Officer – Person who finds homes for evacuated children.

Billets – The homes in which the evacuees stayed.

Blackout – Time when no lights were allowed to be seen.

Blitz – German air raids on Great Britain that took place from 7 September 1940 to 21 May 1941.

CORB – Children's Overseas Reception Board.

Doodlebug – Another name for a V-1 flying bomb.

Evacuate – To send people out of a dangerous area to areas where they will be safe.

Foster Parents – The people looking after the evacuees in their homes.

Incendiary Bomb – A bomb designed to burst into flames when it hits its target.

Kindertransport – A humanitarian mission to help children escape occupied countries by train.

IWM – Imperial War Museum.

LDV – Local Defence Volunteers (later became the Home Guard).

LEA – Lowestoft Evacuees Association.

Luftwaffe – German air force.

Money – The English pound (£) contained 20 shillings (s) each of 12 pennies (d). Two shillings and six pence is written as 2s6d.

Operation Pied Piper – The Government's code name for the evacuation scheme in WW2.

Reception Areas – Areas of the country thought to be safe, to which the evacuees were sent.

Shrapnel – Flying fragments from a shell.

Sirens – Loud sound that acted as a warning of air raids.

'The Evacuee' – The BEA bi-monthly magazine.

The Phoney War – The eight month period between the British declaration of war on 3 September 1939 and the invasion of France and the low countries, by the Germans, on 10 May 1940.

V-1s and V-2s – Flying missiles used against Britain towards the end of WW2.

VE Day – Victory in Europe.

VJ Day – Victory in Japan, thus ending WW2.

WVS – Women's Voluntary Services from 1936 to 1966.

WAAF – Women's Auxiliary Air Force.

DR. ANGELA MUS.
'MUSSO